SELF-AWARENESS FOR WOMEN

A Self-Betterment Journal for Self-Actualization, Balancing Emotions, Forgiveness & Meditation

ANGELA GRACE

CONTENTS

Get Your *BONUS* Manifesting Secret Formula Toolkit	v
Introduction	ix
1. EMPOWER YOUR THOUGHTS, TRANSFORM YOUR LIFE	1
Take a Step Back	3
2. SELF-ACTUALIZATION AND HOW TO CATAPULT TOWARD IT AT THE SPEED OF LIGHT	8
The Emotional Exploration of Self-Awareness	10
3. WAKE UP AND DISCOVER HOW TO LIVE NOW	20
Living in the Present	22
4. TAKING OUT THE TRASH, SPIRITUAL HEALING & THE DISTRIBUTION OF YOUR PRECIOUS ENERGY	27
Setting Healthy Boundaries	31
5. EMOTIONAL INTELLIGENCE, SELF-AWARENESS, AND BALANCING EMOTIONS	36
The Art of Analyzing Yourself	38
6. THE BEAUTY OF MISTAKES AND HOW SCREW-UPS CAN BOOST YOUR SELF-ESTEEM INTO THE STRATOSPHERE	44
A Healthy and Positive Inner Dialogue	45
7. SELF-COMPASSION, SELF-LOVE, AND SELF-FORGIVENESS	50
Easy-to-Follow Exercises	54
8. INNER COURAGE & SELF-RESPECT	61
Reprogramming Yourself	64

9. WHY ALL THE SELF-GROWTH? WHY FIND YOUR DHARMA? WHAT DO YOU REALLY WANT?	69
Destroy Your Distractions	71
10. AMAZING GUIDED MEDITATIONS TO SUPERCHARGE YOUR SELF-AWARENESS	76
Guided Meditation for Self-Realization	76
Guided Meditation for Self-Love	79
Guided Meditation to Forgive Yourself	81
Guided Meditation for Success	83
11. THE 30-MINUTE DAILY EMPOWERMENT RITUAL TO SUPERCHARGE SELF-AWARENESS	86
Self-Awareness Daily Ritual Secret Formula	88
Afterword	95
References	99
Your feedback is valued	103
Your FREE Audiobook is Ready	105

GET YOUR *BONUS*
MANIFESTING SECRET
FORMULA TOOLKIT

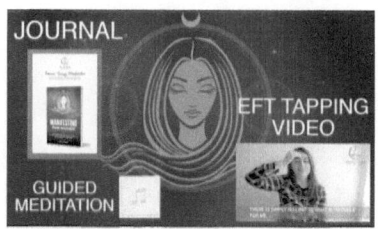

Are you DONE with settling for a mediocre life, wasting precious time, & ready to live your wildest fantasies?

- Hack your brain, boost performance, & release blocks holding you back from greatness
- Awaken this amazing energy to supercharge your manifestations
- Stop wasting what little precious time you have on ineffective methods

1. **Supercharged Manifestation EFT Tapping Video:** Download To Banish Limiting Beliefs & Propel You

Toward Your Dream Life! (Infused with 432 Hz Frequency)
2. **Secret Formula Journal:** Daily manifestation Ritual Done For You, Simply Rinse & Repeat At Home! (You Can Print This Out, Stick On Your Wall, & Cross Off The Days You Complete The Ritual)
3. **Powerful 10 Minute 'Shifting Your reality' Guided Meditation** MP3 Download (Infused with 528 Hz Frequency)
4. ***BONUS*** LOA boosting 10 Minute 'Feminine Energy Awakening' Guided Meditation MP3 Download

Go To This Link To Get Your *BONUS* Manifesting Secret Formula Toolkit:
bit.ly/manifestingforwomen

© **Copyright 2021 - Ascending Vibrations - All rights reserved.**

The content contained within this book may not be reproduced, duplicated or transmitted without direct written permission from the author or the publisher.

Under no circumstances will any blame or legal responsibility be held against the publisher, or author, for any damages, reparation, or monetary loss due to the information contained within this book, either directly or indirectly.

Legal Notice:

This book is copyright protected. It is only for personal use. You cannot amend, distribute, sell, use, quote or paraphrase any part, or the content within this book, without the consent of the author or publisher.

Disclaimer Notice:

Please note the information contained within this document is for educational and entertainment purposes only. All effort has been executed to present accurate, up to date, reliable, complete information. No warranties of any kind are declared or implied. Readers acknowledge that the author is not engaged in the rendering of legal, financial, medical or professional advice. The content within this book has been derived from various sources. Please consult a licensed professional before attempting any techniques outlined in this book.

By reading this document, the reader agrees that under no circumstances is the author responsible for any losses, direct or indirect, that are incurred as a result of the use of the information contained within this document, including, but not limited to, errors, omissions, or inaccuracies.

INTRODUCTION

Most people go through their life without actually having a real purpose. They feel empty inside, trying to complete that void but always missing out on something. It is in our nature as humans to serve a higher purpose, a natural calling. This gives us a sense of accomplishment and accompanies us in our everyday life. As a result, we are happier and healthier. We steer clear of negative emotions and distractions. This is the way we have always been destined to live, so it feels completely natural. Don't you want to feel the same?

In order to embark on this wonderful journey and reveal your higher purpose in life, you first need to discover who you really are. Self-awareness is critical, as it sheds light on the mysteries of your being. Unless you are completely aware of who you are, where you are standing, and what you truly need, you cannot unveil the deepest truths of life. You cannot reveal your inner truth and align with the universe. In other words, self-awareness is the key that unlocks the real beauty in your life through the distractions, the hardships, and the obstacles.

We spend our days surrounded by people who are on autopilot. Perhaps you are feeling the same way too. You wake up in the morning, go about doing your daily tasks, and never sit still. In this way, you never have the chance to evaluate your actions. This prevents you from reaching your fullest potential. It entraps you in a life that can only get you to a certain point and leaves you wanting more. Through the process of self-discovery, though, you are free to explore the vastness of your existence.

There are emotions holding us back, creating physical barriers that we cannot overcome. This leads to feelings of regret, guilt, and hostility towards others. We loathe ourselves for things we have done in the past, although we were meant to show love and cherish ourselves. Therefore, we are unable to expand our life and discover our hidden identities. It seems as if we sabotage ourselves without even realizing that we do. Why would you settle for a life like that when you can have so much more?

By choosing this book, you have taken the first step towards unveiling who you really are. I am so proud of your decision to change the things that don't work for you. I will help you in your endeavor by explaining what you should pay attention to and how to proceed. In my book, you will get all the tools you need for this lovely transformation of your life—from the theoretical background of this earth-shattering philosophy to practical resources to turn to in order to discover your inner self.

MY JOURNEY

It fills me with great content to see that so many amazing women like you have trusted me to guide you through this life-changing process. I have been blessed with so many things in life, one of which is finding my true calling. In the past, I have struggled a great deal to discover my own identity. Most days, I would try to find the motivation to complete my tasks and stay focused on what I had to do. I used to blame myself for lack of concentration and laziness. This is what I thought because I had no idea that the reason for my idleness was deeper and more spiritual.

INTRODUCTION

As I stumbled upon spirituality and energy healing, after a deep conversation with my dear friend Linda, it felt like I had an epiphany. Everything suddenly made sense. I would see clearly what I had to do in life so that I lived to my fullest potential. Over time, I came across the concept of self-awareness, and this is when I knew what I was destined to do my entire life. I wanted to become a spiritual guide, helping others find their path that unfolds their endless possibilities. To be honest, I am so grateful for this opportunity I have been given to do the things I love in my everyday life, avoiding distractions that would only leave me astray.

From then on, the pieces of the puzzle have been completed. I looked deep into my soul, and I saw myself without any lenses. It was just me and my truth. Of course, the process of discovering who you are is not easy. Sometimes it is painful to look at yourself from a distance and realize that you are only human. Nobody is perfect, and this is perfectly fine. I got to accept myself and all my flaws, trying to modify my behavior so that I attracted what I truly deserved. Let me tell you, this journey has made me see things from a new perspective. I was ready to follow my dharma, my higher purpose in life, helping others reach that blissful state.

I have written a lot of books focusing on several aspects of spirituality and self-discovery. Through my work, I have managed to reach out to many people in distress. I have achieved my goal to help others with a guiding compass that leads the way to the life they are entitled to. Books like *Spiritual Cleansing, Energy Healing Made Easy, Protect Your Energy, Crystals Made Easy, Feminine Energy Awakening, Manifesting for Women,* and *Reiki Made Easy* have been created as beacons of light for you and like-minded people with an internal yearning for self-growth.

The Road Less Traveled

In a world where everything seems to be going too fast, it can be difficult to listen to yourself gasping for air. It is much simpler to quiet that internal voice of yours, eventually becoming numb. However, you are not meant to live life like that. You are destined

INTRODUCTION

for greatness. There are amazing things for you to discover as soon as you unravel the mysteries that lie within you. Hopefully, this book leads you exactly where you are supposed to be.

You should not waste any more of your invaluable time. Delve into this endeavor wholeheartedly so that you find the truth. Set out on an adventure that enables you to expand beyond your own limitations until you find your inner balance. Instead of living each of your days wondering how things would be for you, take that first step towards enlightenment. The road less traveled will take you to your destination. It is in your power to take charge of your life today and start living to your fullest potential.

Read along and explore your wonderful self. Live in the present moment, aware of your reality. Get rid of the negativity, clearing out your emotional baggage and making room for the spectacular things to come. Set healthy boundaries in your relationships with others and take a look within you. Boost your emotional intelligence and analyze yourself, as well as others. Find the courage that lies within you to reprogram yourself and self-reflect on your life so far. Initiate a healthy and positive inner dialogue, learning how to trust yourself. Finally, use my guided meditations to accomplish everything you want in life and set a daily empowerment ritual to supercharge your self-awareness.

I am sure you are as excited as I am for the things that are about to follow. Keep on reading, take notes, and get ready to welcome life as it should be. This is going to be a marvelous transformation, so buckle up, and let's get started!

I

EMPOWER YOUR THOUGHTS, TRANSFORM YOUR LIFE

What is the definition of a "habit"? Simply put, it is a set of unconscious thoughts, behaviors, and emotions that are acquired through repetition. You have done something so many times in your life, making your body know better how to do that than your own mind. A brain is the record of your past, including memories that have been associated with specific emotions. Every time you wake up and start thinking about these memories, you are already thinking in the past. When you think about your problems, you bring to the surface memories that are related to negative emotions. Therefore, you cannot help but feel unhappy and unfulfilled.

How you think and how you feel create your state of being, defining your very existence. This brings you to a vicious cycle when the familiar past becomes the foreseeable future. When you wake up in the morning and prepare your coffee, wash your face, and drive to work following the same routine, you basically comply with a set program. Instead of exercising free will, you have substituted it with a programmable day. What you need to do is change the way you think, slow down, and reprogram your mind.

Long-term memories are built up by high emotional past experiences. When you go through a traumatic event, your mind automatically tells you to recall that event and relive that trauma. This happens because you want to be prepared for similar things that might happen in your life, to avoid experiencing the same frustration. By living in this state of negative anticipation, you actually expect the worst-case scenario to play out in your life. All that happens is based on past experiences. So out of the endless possibilities out there, you choose the worst one due to the fact that it is compatible with what you have already experienced.

As a result, you are conditioning your body into a state of fear. From a biological standpoint, this process reveals that you have not been able to change all this time through reprogramming your mind to pursue and anticipate better outcomes. Even if this is bad for you, you tend to stick with the negative emotions. Why do you do that? Because you have become accustomed to them. You know them, and therefore you expect them to come into your life. However, in the long run, these negative emotions only reaffirm your limitations and prevent you from reaching your highest purpose. You might feel as though they are protecting you, but in fact, all they do is bring you down and create a wall that keeps you confined.

The best way to predict your future is for you to create it. You should create it not from the known but from the unknown. Take a step back and analyze the way you act. How do you behave towards yourself, and how do you treat others? How do you react to certain situations in life? If you look closely, you will realize that you have created several behavioral patterns that determine your being. You use those patterns to help you decode reality and act accordingly. Yet, problematic behaviors are not meant to be repeated again and again.

Once you decide to change the way you behave, this is going to be quite uncomfortable for you. This makes perfect sense, as you will be stepping out of your comfort zone and doing things that you are not familiar with. You need to be aware of the fact that your body will attempt to hold you back, forcing you to return to a familiar state. If you are determined to pursue a different outcome and get out of a negative feeling, your physical being will resist that change. Unless you are strong enough to hold your ground and persist in your decision to change, your effort will not be successful.

TAKE A STEP BACK

Negative thinking and unwanted thoughts can be extremely debilitating, as they consume your energy and leave you exhausted. They are pointless since they do not provide you with any solutions to the things that take up space in your mind. Therefore, you need to steer clear of those negative thoughts. However, they tend to be persistent and really take up a lot of your time. There are moments when you simply cannot complete any given task because you have been crippled by such thoughts.

Clearing unhelpful, negative, and depressing inner dialogue is of the essence if you are truly determined to improve your life. Otherwise, you will be spending your days frozen. You will continuously stress yourself over things that do not help you in any way. They do not offer a way for you to escape. Once you do clear out unhelpful and negative thoughts and inner dialogue, though, you will make space for self-realization to grow. So it is crucial that you know how to silence these voices from within and channel your mind into a more productive, healthier mindset.

One simple yet effective way to stop negative thoughts is to ask yourself if what you are thinking is useful. Are all these thoughts that you are having helpful? Do they improve your current situation, even in the slightest manner? This question will put you in control of your thoughts. Once you evaluate these negative thoughts, you will see that they are actually useless. They do not hold any real value, and they only make you feel miserable. If you let them take control of your life, you give away your power.

For example, there will be times when you are feeling depressed about something bad that has happened to you. Perhaps you got into a fight with a friend or you broke up with your relationship. Maybe you had a bad day at the office, and your supervisor yelled at you. Whatever it is, it is going to trigger a lot of negative thoughts. You will be spending your day thinking of the following: *"I am not good enough. I don't deserve anything. I am not worthy of being loved. Everyone around me hates me. I drive all people away from me. I am incapable of having a meaningful, honest relationship."*

As soon as these thoughts creep in, you need to ask yourself: *"Are these thoughts useful to me right now? Are they helping me with my situation?"* The obvious answer is that they are not helpful at all. They do not help you with your situation. In fact, what they do is to make things even worse. Now that you have clarified that this type of thinking is pointless, you give yourself permission to let go of these thoughts. You get rid of them since they harm you and prevent your growth. This is a deliberate decision you have made based on your honest answer.

At the same time, this simple trick motivates you to take action. You can choose to remain consumed in your own negative thoughts. However, you should know that this is not going to help you in any way. Instead, you can choose to take action and change what is bothering you in your life. When you become conscious of a problem, you can fight it off more easily. By empowering your thoughts and controlling them, you can modify your behavior based on facts and observation.

Dedicate a few moments in writing some things down that you want to change in your life. They can be relevant to the way you behave, the way you act, the way you feel, or how you interpret several situations. Do you feel sorry for yourself? Do you lack confidence? Are you constantly worried about what others might think of you? That all represents the consciousness of a victim. You don't want to be a victim in your life. Similarly, you can analyze the emotions you live by. People tend to live in guilt and not even realize it.

When you finish with your self-evaluation, visualize the things you wish to see in your life. Picture them in detail as they will fire and wire your brain. Rehearse those feelings stemming from happy and fulfilling situations so that you prepare your body and mind for them. It is important that you teach your body emotionally to experience what your life should be before it manifests. Over time, you will see that your existence aligns with these new thoughts and responds to them in a positive manner.

Practice living in your desired state on a daily basis, and you will soon find yourself attracting the things that you want in life. Although it might seem impossible right now, I promise that your entire existence will be transformed through this simple yet highly effective tool triggered by your mind. Enjoy these wonderful emotions that are going to burst within you and flood you with happiness, accomplishment, and abundance. Give thanks for these feelings as you are receiving the greatest gifts in life.

Let Go of Worry

Worry is a kind of fear. It is not the fear of an imminent threat because you do not have a direct stimulant driving this feeling. When you are walking down the street, it is dark outside and you are heading towards an isolated territory, you get a sense of fear regarding what threats may be there for you. This is an entirely different situation. Worry is the feeling you get out of a fear about something that has been imagined. It is the fear about something that has not happened, but you imagine it as a potential threat in the future.

If you are wondering about the benefits derived from worry, I am afraid that you will come up empty. This is because worry is never helpful. When a person feels depressed or angry, worry escalates those negative emotions and brings them out of proportion. In that sense, it is counter-productive. Why would you waste your time worrying about the future when you can choose to live in the present moment and experience the only tangible reality?

Everything else is a figment of your imagination. You must find a way to focus on the present rather than think about the future and end up worrying about it. Self-awareness is critical in your endeavor to interpret the world and see reality objectively. You need to look around you and see what is happening in your life. Catch yourself worrying and try to rationalize. Is this feeling justified? Does it help you in your current state? I am guessing you will realize that it is, in fact, holding you back, preventing you from taking action in the first place.

It is essential that you fully comprehend the dimension of worry in order to deal with it effectively. You should open your eyes and understand that you are safe right now. At this very moment, nothing bad has happened. Consequently, you need not worry. It cannot hurt you in any way. Once you have found yourself in a place where you are not influenced by this negative emotion, you need to take a step forward and shield yourself against it.

You can do that through a powerful self-reflection. Encourage yourself and take positive action. Using affirmations will help you get past this discomforting feeling. Tell yourself that you are worthy of taking risks without the fear of failure. Repeat that you have been in similar situations before in your life, and they have not been able to break you. Alternatively, you can distract yourself and take your focus from looking inward into the world. Take a walk or chat with a friend of yours, hit the gym, or cook a nice meal for you and your loved ones. As a result, your mind will be distracted, and you will have the opportunity to act without worry lurking in the dark.

Sensing the inner body or the inner feeling of your energy can snap you into the present moment where you can dwell and make conscious choices in your life. These choices will not be based on automatic emotional reaction. This can be achieved through yoga, meditation and pranayama (breathing practices/breathwork). Later on in the book, I will discuss some powerful present-day coping mechanisms for you to utilize. For example, emotional freedom technique (EFT) tapping has been proven exceptionally helpful in clearing out negative energy and overcoming limiting beliefs.

You should focus on taking it one day at a time rather than filling your mind with potential threats that undermine your future. You cannot be overwhelmed by "what if" situations. When something takes place, you see it and you evaluate it. As such, you are able to react in a way that aligns with your mentality and your lifestyle. Until then, there is no point in tormenting yourself. Don't lose sleep over an invisible fear.

This doesn't mean that you should not organize your life or make plans for the future. You should get ready and rehearse possible outcomes so that you are not taken by surprise. Still, don't worry about negative outcomes regarding things that have not yet occurred. It will take you nowhere, and it is going to make your life a lot harder. You deserve to make the most of your mind by letting go of things that are out of your control.

2

SELF-ACTUALIZATION AND HOW TO CATAPULT TOWARD IT AT THE SPEED OF LIGHT

Self-actualization is an amazing term, although unfortunately, many people seem to disregard its value. Introduced by Kurt Goldstein in 1939, the term initially referred to the tendency of people to actualize their capacities (Sullivan, 2019). However, Abraham Maslow was the one to clearly describe the very essence of self-actualization. It is the drive for autonomy, development, and growth. He saw self-actualization as a constant motivation for growth. It is a never-ending process as humans struggle to achieve greatness through an ongoing journey towards reaching their end goal.

While creating the famous "hierarchy of needs" as a pyramid, Maslow defined the various needs that a person wishes to cover in life. Starting at the bottom, there are the basic physiological needs that have to be met. These include food, water, a place to sleep, and rest. Moving upwards, there is the need for safety. A little further above, we find the needs for belonging and love. Esteem needs come next, featuring the need to accomplish things in life and gain prestige. Finally, at the top of the pyramid lies the need for self-actualization (McLeod, 2020).

Carl Rogers is Maslow's peer and also referred to self-actualization in his "person-centered therapy." According to that theory, an individual's identity is formed by a complex group of subjective beliefs about themselves. It is the motivation for people to be healthy and develop, finding a true purpose in life. This is a true need for growth. Rogers took it a step further and claimed that self-actualization is the fabric that blends everything together. This is people's only drive to expand, grow, and evolve (Davis, 2019).

There is a slight misconception that has been baffling people as to what self-actualization really is. Some people think that it is what drives us to change. In that sense, it would not be able to hold its ground as the epicenter of self-discovery. However, it is a process that targets our higher self. We don't want to change ourselves in the process. What we do is simply make the best choices that are based on who we really are.

Others describe a self-actualized person as narcissistic, egoistic, and self-centered. This could not be further from the truth. It is a fact that by doing some deep soul-searching, you become more conscious of yourself and the environment. This is a part of the learning process to believe in yourself, getting rid of any pressure to conform with society. You cannot expand if you are focused solely on yourself. Still, this doesn't mean that you act selfishly or you wish to undermine others.

In a nutshell, being self-actualized refers to living to your full potential. This is not some sort of luxury, as some people might argue. On the contrary, it reflects one of the core needs that each person has. If you do not live up to your full potential, it is going to rot you from inside. You are bound to develop neuroses and be dysfunctional in your life. Just like you need vitamins and nutrients to avoid deficiencies, you also need self-actualization to maintain optimal psychological and physical health.

Self-actualization has been directly associated with what being human means. You owe it to yourself to be passionate and driven. It is in your hands to change the course of your life, aiming higher and higher. By discovering your true self, you get to live exactly the way you have been destined to. Enjoy a positively charged life, appreciate every moment, and join others in their quest towards self-improvement. A wonderful journey lies ahead.

THE EMOTIONAL EXPLORATION OF SELF-AWARENESS

It all boils down to self-awareness. You need to know who you are and act accordingly. Unless you fully comprehend your identity, you cannot expect to thrive and grow spiritually. It is an amazing emotional exploration that leads you to your end goal, finding yourself. In order for you to reach that higher purpose of your life and discover your very essence, you should retrospect and delve deeper into your psyche.

Here, I am going to lay down a list of the things that a self-actualized person does in life. These characteristics can serve as a checklist so that you identify where you stand. A self-actualized person will most likely do the following:

- Have a superior perception of reality, looking at things more objectively than most
- Be accepting of themselves as well as others and the environment
- Be more spontaneous, refusing to allow rules to dictate how they feel
- Have a better focus on problems in life, as they will not be absorbed in the way they feel
- Experience increased detachment from things, meaning that a self-actualized person won't cling to things
- Enjoy privacy and solitude, feeling great while spending time on their own
- Have a higher sense of individuality and autonomy

- Assume full responsibility for the course of their life so far, not trying to put the blame on others
- Be world citizens rather than slaves to their culture
- Be absolutely comfortable being themselves without requesting any approval from others
- Have a good grasp of reality since they value the facts and the truth over dogma
- Have appreciation and emotional richness
- Be open to new experiences
- Love humanity, as they accept the fact that they are part of a species
- Enjoy improved interpersonal relationships
- Be democratic characters instead of dictating their beliefs and enforcing them on others
- Be creative and authentic in their everyday life
- Have deep knowledge and understanding of who they are, even about things that most would choose to ignore
- Believe in unity and integration
- Build up skills and talents as they know where to focus on for optimal results
- Experience positivity in all aspects of their life, since they are positively driven
- Do things they love to do, not forcing themselves to do things they have to
- Enjoy every second and appreciate the moment
- Don't judge, avoiding getting consumed by the negative energy that comes with such bad habits
- Be more loving; although they need less love, they tend to give more
- Be open minded and accept the fact that they are not always right
- Have better psychological health than others
- Have a sense of mission in their life and a purpose to fulfil

- Understand the importance of work and be proud of their professional achievements
- Wish to improve the world and make it a better place
- Admit their mistakes and do their best to rectify them
- Be disciplined and align that with their own satisfactions, believing that duty equals pleasure
- Don't lash out but express their aggression more healthily
- Move towards things so as to get joy from things in life, not misery
- Live in the present
- Make more conscious decisions

A self-actualized person has a set of noble values to live their life by, including truth, beauty, goodness, uniqueness, wholeness, simplicity, richness, playfulness, and justice. These are not the only values, of course. However, they do set the bar high. They elevate that person's soul and mind by instilling positive energy on all levels. Self-actualization is all about optimizing your true self—getting rid of negativity and everything that comes along with this poisonous feeling.

Take a moment and reflect on yourself. Do you have these characteristics? I am sure that you have seen quite a few traits that match your own personality. However, even if you don't, you will have the chance to enhance them through some simple yet greatly effective exercises later on in this book. This is going to be a wonderful challenge, so get ready to nail it!

30 Tips on How to Get Started with Self-Actualization

I know it might seem chaotic at first to dive right in to pursuing self-actualization. You have no tangible evidence that can guide you through the process, which may hinder your progress from the very beginning. In order to avoid that and lose focus on what is truly important, here is a list of the 30 hottest tips to get you started.

- Find your life purpose: How do you want to contribute to humanity? What is your purpose in life? It is essential that you find that out as soon as possible. When you do, master that domain. Optimize your skills and organize your life in a way that promotes constant growth. You should be passionate about your life. Most people torment themselves as they grind through their work. By finding your life purpose, you will feel liberated from all that ordeal. This discovery will give you high-quality, long-lasting motivation to try harder.
- Reprogram your subconscious mind: It takes time to reprogram your mind on a subconscious level. However, this is what you need to achieve greatness. You can choose the strategies that best appeal to you. Affirmations and visualizations have been proven to work wonders, getting you to the root of the beliefs you have. Change the patterns you don't like. Analyze your fears and insecurities so that you can fight them off.
- Practice meditation: Meditation is an essential part of your journey towards self-awareness and growth. It will transform your life. Incorporate it into your daily routine, and never let go. Mindfulness meditation with labeling is an excellent form of meditation. In this case, you can use labels when meditating. Just picture writing something that defines each thought on a post-it note. This will allow you to hear, see, feel, and deconstruct your sensory field. This is fundamental in breaking down the concepts and fantasies your mind is creating. Through meditation, you reach those parts of your psyche that are too hard to reach otherwise.
- Concentration: Although at first you may confuse it with meditation, it is an entirely different concept. Most people nowadays lack the ability to stay focused, affected by modern technology in the most evident manner. It is

true that you cannot sit down for a few minutes without feeling on edge. This prevents you from contemplating or meditating. You lack focus. Therefore, it is of paramount importance that you build a concentration practice to turn to for help.

- Self-inquiry: This will help you reach the truth on all levels. By asking yourself and searching for the right answers, you are on your path towards enlightenment. See why things are good for you and adjust your behavioral patterns. In this way, you will discover things you never knew about yourself.
- Journaling: This is especially crucial for those of you who are just starting out on their endeavor. You need to get a notebook that you enjoy using. Dedicate 5-10 minutes every day to write about what you want in your life. What are your greatest fears? What is your life vision? Analyze your past and your future. It doesn't really matter what you write, as long as you do that consistently. Over time, you will be amazed by the results.
- Learn the theory: Take notes and learn everything you possibly can about the theoretical pillars of self-actualization. It is essential that you identify how to proceed. Could you ever operate on a person without any theoretical background? The same applies to personal development without any guide. You can attend courses on the matter as they are a wealth of information.
- Do your research: You can study spiritual traditions to comprehend their wisdom. Stay away from dogma, though. Furthermore, there are masterful teachers eager to help you out in your research, as well as inspire you. All in all, do your research and combine different sources of information to get the facts straight.
- Attend retreats: Have you ever considered joining a self-

growth retreat? They are amazing and provide you with all the necessary resources to develop your self-actualization strategy. Otherwise, a solo retreat is a wonderful idea. You basically find a quiet place where you can relax and remain isolated for at least 12 hours a day. Remember that you should be doing nothing other than hearing your thoughts and reaching out to your higher self.

- Psychedelics: This might sound controversial or provocative. However, I have no intention of this advice being either. It is true that certain psychedelics are legal, and they can be extremely helpful in your attempt to break down the walls you have been building. Always use them in a healthy, respectful, and legal manner. By being responsible, you can achieve amazing results specifically for personal development purposes.
- End poisonous relationships: Dysfunctional and toxic relationships need to go. Of course, some of them can be salvaged. Cut out the toxic ones, as they are robbing you of your highest potential. When you see hope, try harder. Learn how to communicate properly and let go of your ego. Don't use your relationships for selfish needs. This is toxifying your relationship, so identify where you are scheming and manipulating.
- Radical honesty: Are you ready for the truth? You hide so much from everyone in life, even from yourself, that it makes you feel a huge burden. Simply by choosing to be brutally honest with yourself and others in life, you will feel much better.
- Make new friends: Well, most people form friendships in their early childhood or adolescence. There are those who make new friends at college or at their workplace. Still, you need to be strategic and conscious. You should find like-minded people like entrepreneurs, spiritual

guides, or people with higher consciousness. Once you start these new friendships, you will see a boost in your own motivation to grow.
- Try out neuro linguistic programming (NLP): NLP techniques can be quite useful when targeting a modification of behavior. Such techniques include visualizations, pseudo-hypnosis, reprogramming your subconscious self, and rewiring your behavioral patterns (Kandola, 2017).
- Shadow work: Another technique that can work for you is shadow work. In this case, you identify the repressed aspects of your psyche—your deepest fears and the things that you have oppressed. Instead of doing therapy, you do the same on your own.
- Lucid dreams, astral projection, reiki, acupuncture, and chakra cleaning: All these new age techniques that can help you find your inner balance. They are helpful in cleansing your energy centers and removing any blockages, leaving room for self-growth.
- Clean up your diet: This is really up to you. There is not a single diet to follow. It can be paleo, vegan, vegetarian, or even a raw food diet. You simply need to cut down on artificial foods, overly processed items, and junk. Aim at wholesome food, and you will start feeling like a million dollars.
- Physical activity: Staying active is essential if you are determined to reach your highest potential. Yoga offers the best results, as it combines physical and spiritual benefits. Hatha yoga is a great option, achieving energy blockage release. You can also try out old school yoga. Pranayama and kundalini yoga are exceptional, along with mantras to purify your energy centers and lead to awakenings and physical healing.
- Proper breathing and holotropic breathwork: Even

though most people do not really pay attention to the way they breathe, they sabotage themselves. It is crucial to realize that your breathing so far has been shallow. On the contrary, you need to opt for deep breathing that fills your lungs and stomach with air. Holotropic breathing in particular can release emotional baggage.

- Reichian therapy: Physical exercises are always effective. Reichian therapy specifically has to do with physical exercises that will allow the release of negative energy from your body.
- Body awareness: Being aware of your body is necessary. You should comprehend how you hold yourself. Check your posture and feel the tension. Try to identify where this is coming from, along with the limitations of your energy. So many diseases stem from that lack of body awareness.
- Clean up your information intake: You would think that the more, the merrier. However, this is not the case for your information digest. TV, YouTube, news, politics, gossip, tabloids, and all that garbage can be extremely addictive. Be mindful of what you receive, and cut out any unnecessary distractions.
- Eliminate addictions: Although you may consider them harmless, alcohol, junk food, coffee, smoking, porno, and video games limit the time you have for self-actualization. Even subtle addictions need to be dealt with. They are sneaky, and you do not even know you are doing them—for instance, chasing success and love, judging, perfectionism, debating, or criticizing. Cold turkey is always the best approach when dealing with addictions.
- Experience more: Travel, interact with new people, and have deep conversations with more people. See the complexity of life. Be open to new experiences, and do

not fear the unknown. There are so many new things in life waiting for you to explore.
- Socialization skills: Even though solitude can be beneficial at times, you cannot isolate yourself permanently. Develop your social skills so that you interact with people more fluently. Dating skills are also part of socialization.
- Relaxation and entertainment: Find new ways to relax and entertain yourself. These should be healthy and not toxic ways that poison your life and distract you from your purpose. Some of the best options for you to consider are sports, activities that have to do with nature, meditation, and voluntary work.
- Get your stuff in order: Organize everything, structure your day, and settle your affairs. Do not leave anything unfinished, as this drags you down and prevents your inner growth. A simple example would be to set automatic bill payments. This will free up a lot of your time on a monthly basis, allowing you to commit to higher explorations.
- Minimize your lifestyle: Minimalism is a great concept in life. Nevertheless, modern society has led you astray. You don't have enough time to do nothing. You do many things every day, constantly drowning and gasping for air. This is wrong. You need to take a step back and indulge in utter serenity. Soak in life, and don't get distracted by anything.
- Find a life coach: This is a tip that not everyone is able to enjoy. Of course, when you are young and have money issues, you should not trouble yourself with such an option. However, there are times when a life coach makes sense. You can work with them intensively, especially if you can afford that sort of investment.
- Neurofeedback training: Finally, you can try out

neurofeedback training. In this manner, you can learn how to control brain events by using conscious feedback in real time. Electrodes are attached to your head. You use training routines to synchronize your mind's work, and gradually you channel your brain accordingly.

3

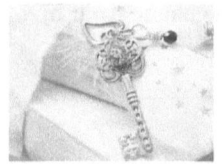

WAKE UP AND DISCOVER HOW TO LIVE NOW

Mindfulness is all about living in the present. Have you ever been caught up in a situation where you almost seem like you are functioning on auto-pilot? It is true that we all live hectic lives, filled with tasks and obligations we simply cannot ignore. However, this only distracts us from our goals. There is no point in maximizing your life, creating even more of these tasks and obligations. They will not offer you anything in return other than pure stress and anxiety along the way.

Self-awareness is closely associated with the concept of mindfulness. When you truly want to discover what lies beneath the surface, you need to get rid of the distractions. Mindfulness offers you the opportunity to experience the moment, without judgment and without any distortive lenses. It is a state of being when you appreciate the dimension of stillness and get to see what is there. If you want to explore your roots, then you should practice mindfulness through meditations and other activities leading to the same amazing path.

In a world where sounds echo in the background, being still might seem impossible to achieve at first glance. Nevertheless, you can practice and find ways to quiet your mind. You can train yourself to create a distance from everything that is going on around you, experiencing that magical stillness. Instead of sabotaging yourself by amplifying the noise, it would be great if you could turn it off altogether.

Through self-awareness, you are bound to be braver and wiser. Even though you may feel terrified of what you are about to discover, it is essential to see yourself holistically. You can dig deeper and find out your behavioral patterns, your motivations, your strengths, and weaknesses. Over time, you will have the opportunity to practice for goodness and grace without expecting to be perfect. Once you have the knowledge of who you are eventually you can control your destiny.

In the process, you will be able to boost your emotional intelligence and carve your own path to follow in life. Although it is great to accept yourself and love unconditionally, this is not a static thing. On the contrary, it is fluid and ever-changing. If you are determined to have specific outcomes in your life, then you need to change your ways. Unless you know who you are, though, you cannot comprehend what it takes for you to modify yourself.

In this book, you will find all the necessary tools you need to reach that point of self-awareness. Rather than reminiscing about those times of the past or daydreaming about what you want to achieve in the future, you will unlock the magic of the present moment. Why let these moments pass you by? Why struggle for something that has not come yet or worry over things that have already been done?

LIVING IN THE PRESENT

What does "living in the present" actually mean? Many people would argue that it involves modifying your life. Yet, it is exactly the opposite. You need to connect with your presence in your daily life. This can be a challenge. Rather than wishing things were different in your everyday routine, try to accept them as they come. Life is filled with challenges, and this is great. Nothing comes easy, but why would it?

Let go of the unconscious assumption that there should be no problems or difficulties. Accept everything that arises in the moment. There may be times when you feel worn out, disappointed, or even saddened by the events in your life. These are parts of the path that you need to follow. There is no reason why you should reject these difficulties simply because they do not match your wishful thinking.

It is alright to be afraid of what you are going to see as soon as you observe your reflections in the mirror. This process can be painful and overwhelming at times. Nonetheless, you should comprehend that something is more important than fear. Insight, authenticity, and self-awareness are elements that allow you to reach your higher self. It takes courage to endure the intense pain that comes with self-discovery.

There are things you are not proud of, but you have to accept them. They are part of who you are. By doing so, you will be able to eliminate these negative thoughts you have been drowning with.

Humans are imperfect. No one can argue with that. There are those who overestimate their contributions. They think they are better than what they are. Others underestimate themselves. It is impressive that on average, women tend to underestimate how they perform at work. At the same time, they appear to be slightly more effective as leaders. So why does that happen?

It goes back to the idea of avoiding arrogance and embracing humility. Women think that by praising themselves, they come off as selfish and mean. They become bitter and resentful. Since they do not want to brag about their accomplishments, they choose silence instead. Yet, this can be a slippery slope. You should never ignore your strengths because they define who you are. Do not neglect your uniqueness, as this will allow others to do the same.

Another aspect of self-awareness is that you get to understand others too. Empathy is a wonderful quality, as it enables you to fully comprehend your peers and those around you. It makes you see more clearly and prevents you from judging others too soon. More than that, through self-awareness you get the chance to see how others perceive you. This is equally inspiring, as it unfolds great mysteries that would otherwise baffle you for a long time.

Before moving forward, it is worth asking yourself if you think you are self-aware right now. Don't force the answer. Then ask those around you if they think the same about themselves. The answers will shock you. Most people will be certain that they are aware of their being. They will think that they don't have to waste time, money or energy in self-discovery. However, the vast majority of people out there lack that awareness. They might believe that they know where they stand and what they are made of, but the truth proves them wrong.

It goes much deeper than knowing how much you weigh, what color your eyes are, how much money you make, or how tall you are. Discovering yourself encapsulates every single truth about your personality, your motivations, your goals and your anticipations, your talents, your soft spots, and the traits that make you special. It also includes your fears and complexes, your dysfunctional patterns, as well as the things that you are bad at and wish you could change. Negative emotions such as envy and jealousy, feelings of inferiority, and vengeance are also included in this self-discovery process.

No matter how painful and demanding it can be, becoming more self-aware will literally transform your life completely. It will show you a clear, objective perspective of your life, without any sugar-coating that might lead you astray. You may feel that some things are better left unsaid. Yet, this only lets you reach a certain point in your being. Unless you are ready to face the ugly truth, you cannot really expect to change it towards being the best you can be. This will initially shock you, but over time it will be therapeutic and cleansing.

If you are about to embark on this wonderful experience of self-awareness, you might find yourself confused as to how to begin. This is why I have included a few pointers on how to become more self-aware below. Devote the time and energy required so that you maximize the benefits derived from knowing yourself. Don't just scratch the surface. Delve deeper, even if it scares you. After having reached a point of unveiling things about yourself you have never considered, persist in your endeavor and try harder.

5+1 Pointers on How to Become More Self-Aware

Below you can see some of the best things you can do when getting started on your journey towards self-awareness. By following these pointers, you will gradually clear out any misconceptions about yourself. It will take some time to get there, but the outcome will definitely compensate you. Self-discovery is far easier when you know where to begin. Incorporate these strategies into your daily routine and discover the realms of your being.

- Daily self-reflection: It is important to see who you are through your own eyes. Start by writing down the accomplishments that make you proud, as well as the qualities you value most about yourself. Take a moment to think about your childhood. What made you happy as a child, and what has changed since then? Furthermore, dedicate some time to evaluate yourself as a leader. If you do that for 15 minutes each day, you will gain a much better understanding of who you really are.

- Keep a journal: Even though you might think journaling is a waste of time, in reality, it is of paramount importance to you. When you write down your thoughts, they become much clearer. These thoughts are also useful to read afterwards when you are in a different state of mind. If you are wondering what you should write, begin with how you feel. What have you achieved during the day? Have you been successful or not? You can do that every night before going to bed. As you move forward, you can also write about how you can achieve more in life.

- Meditate: When you meditate, you enjoy precious moments of peaceful reflection. When drifting away from the harsh reality and the chaotic everyday life, you come across questions that actually matter. If you are still hesitant about devoting time to meditate, keep in mind that you are already doing that. When you are washing the dishes, going to church, or jogging, you focus on the present moment and clear out all other thoughts.

- Personality tests: There are several personality and psychometric tests available for you to take so as to understand your characteristics. When compared to others, these characteristics form your personality and eventually shape who you are. Don't be afraid of those tests, as there are no right or wrong answers. You can take them periodically in order to track your progress and evaluate your journey so far.

- Ask for feedback: Ask people around you to share the qualities that they value most about you. You should be looking for open and critical perspectives. Their honest opinion matters, as it allows you to see how others perceive who you are. This will reveal a lot of things about you that you have been missing out on, even when self-reflecting. It is important to let them know that they are helping you. Otherwise, they may feel compelled to lie. When you see that several answers overlap, these are the truths that you should take into consideration as productive feedback.

- Flash cards: This can be tricky but highly rewarding as a tool. Prepare some flashcards where you write down different aspects of your life. As you pick one of those flashcards, try to be honest and answer if your performance on that specific aspect is average, below, or above average. If you run this experiment with others, you will see that most people feel they are smarter, better at work, better leaders, better drivers, and better friends. Even though this can be true at times, it is a widespread phenomenon for people to believe they are above average in everything. An oxymoron is that the least competent individuals tend to be the most confident ones about their capabilities. Set your ego aside and answer truthfully.

4

TAKING OUT THE TRASH, SPIRITUAL HEALING & THE DISTRIBUTION OF YOUR PRECIOUS ENERGY

As we grow up, we learn how to conform to what society dictates. Our family is the first example of social integration for us, and we learn how to comply with its set of rules. If we are good and obey those rules, we are rewarded. Otherwise, we receive punishment, and we are told never to do that again. Since we are raised in this family, we take everything for granted and gradually learn how to mimic behaviors that are not our own. We have been programmed to act in a certain way, and we don't even question our actions. So when we are talking about free will, we really need to look into the way we have been brought up to act.

This is called "domestication." As we get older, we tend to follow the same behavioral patterns in life. However, sometimes we realize that these patterns don't actually work for us. This is where we try hard to change them because they have been imprinted on us through all these years of observation. We might succeed, or we might fail, but the truth is that these patterns have defined us so far, and they represent a huge part of our being. It all stems from the recollection of our childhood and how we behaved back then. Although you may believe that you are not affected by your early memories, it is inevitable for this to happen. In most cases, this is beneficial to you and your course of life. Still, there are moments when you simply find yourself trapped in these memories of the past.

Become conscious of your inner child. We all do, and many suffer from that. A wound can be created from early childhood and torment you for life. Even if you do not have any recollection of such a traumatic experience, it doesn't mean that it is not there. Ever since you were little, you had certain needs. If those needs were either neglected or unmet, you probably have a wound that has followed you all your life. Again, you don't need to have that memory of this past experience.

It is important to remember that you were a child at the time of the wound. This means that the specific circumstances leading to your traumatic experience are quite different from those you would have right now in your life. Even if something appears to be trivial as an adult, back then it would mean an entirely different thing. Try to look at this with the eyes of a child so as to better understand your trauma.

A great hint towards realizing there is some sort of unresolved conflict in your childhood is the fact that you get triggered by particular incidents. A trigger is a disproportionate reaction to something small that is happening now in your current life. For instance, have you ever found yourself reacting way too much over something unimportant? To me, a trigger was an untidy kitchen. Every time I went into the kitchen and found it dirty with dishes piling up in the sink, I would lash out. Of course, it is not pleasant to clean up after a full day at the office. Still, shouting and crying did not quite comply with the gravity of the situation.

I am certain that you have already spotted similar triggers in your life. If you have, it is worth taking the time to analyze what they are associated with. Listen to your thoughts as you have this trigger. What are they referring to? You will be surprised by the results. In fact, chances are that you have never paid attention to these thoughts up until now. These thoughts can be similar to the following: *"Why did she do that? Why didn't he consider me? Why do my parents not love me? Am I invisible? Don't they listen to what I have to say? Why did she ignore my needs? Why did he have to work all the time?"*

This will start to make sense now. When you were just a kid and depended on your family, you created a network of emotional associations. Your critical thinking was shaped through observation and empirical data. If you wanted to spend time with your parents sitting around the family table and enjoying a nice meal, and your parents were absent a lot due to their hectic schedule, an untidy kitchen might represent that past wound. You are feeling neglected again based on what you experienced as a child.

These triggers are huge red flags you should pay attention to in order to decode the meaning of past traumas. If you want to heal your inner child, you need to address the problem and then aim to eliminate it. Once you get to the root of the problem, you will be able to deal with it properly. The best way to do so is to ask your inner child what it takes to resolve the situation. In my former example, I needed to be considered as part of a loving family. I wanted to feel the presence of those dear to me in a safe and secure environment.

By understanding what has caused the trigger, I was now able to change the way I felt about this specific event. An untidy kitchen would no longer represent my parents' lack of time and consideration towards me. I would go and clean the kitchen for a while so that it looked spotlessly clean, which would make me happy. Then, I would reward myself for this behavior by doing something that I love. Most probably, this would be a walk in the park or a mindfulness meditation for a few moments. That allowed me to heal my inner child completely and move forward.

It is essential that you heal your inner child so that you do not carry around your past traumas in every single aspect of your life.

This would mean that you no longer experience growth. You sit there and contract rather than expand. A great way to achieve that healing is through EFT tapping. EFT deals with the trauma on a fundamental level. In essence, you need to offer your inner child what you never got in the past. This will help you feel better and resolve any emotional issues associated with this experience.

Start tapping on the external part of your palm, repeating the following affirmations: *"I choose to love my inner child. I choose to love and accept all of myself. I choose to send love to my inner child. I choose to deeply and completely love and accept myself."* Continue tapping on the top of your head, your forehead, the third eye and each side of your eyes, your cheekbones, upper lip, and chin. I am guessing you are already feeling better simply by elevating your energy.

"That little me who never got what she needed, I want her to know that I love and accept her for who she is. She is an amazing person, and she can do anything she wants in life. There are no limits to her growth. She will have my unconditional love, as this is her birthright." Keep on tapping on your neckline, the center of your chest and under your armpits and then start over. *"She doesn't have to do anything to earn my love. If she makes a mistake, I will not be mad. It is perfectly alright. I accept my little me, even though I never got acceptance. I picture holding her in my arms and telling her that everything is fine now. I protect her, and I give her reassurance and approval. I let her know that she is accepted and that she is perfect just the way she is."*

A third repetition of EFT tapping should follow. *"I am loving to myself and therefore I am loving to my inner child. I treat my inner child well because I treat myself well. I am kind and compassionate towards myself. I am clearing the trauma and the pain, making sure that it leaves my body. I don't have to endure this suffering anymore. It feels good to let go of this trauma. I am so excited to be stepping into a new relationship with myself. I am no longer afraid."*

Take a deep breath and relax. It is great if you can picture yourself as a child throughout this session. It will help you gain a better perspective of your endeavor to heal your inner child. Ultimately, this EFT tapping method allows you to treat yourself well. When you are on the verge of beating yourself up, imagine that child and how she would feel about that. By organizing your inward energy and your thoughts, you get in an effective state of concentration. With so many competing interests not only inwardly in your mind but outwardly through the environment, you must use conscious (being in the present) concentration and reprogram yourself.

SETTING HEALTHY BOUNDARIES

We as humans are meant to interact with others, forming meaningful relationships that help us move forward. Nevertheless, sometimes we get surrounded by people who project their negative energy towards us and leave us desperately yearning for help. Have you ever felt drained of your energy right after having returned from hanging out with a friend? Although you would expect to feel exactly the opposite, the truth is that you ended up feeling worse than you did before meeting them. This is a hint that the person you have become friends with is toxic. The sooner you remove them from your friends' list, the better.

I know this is easier said than done. There are people who have always been by your side, and still, they have a negative impact on your life. Some people are family members and so your bonds are too hard to break. Still, you should take action. Otherwise, you will be sucked into a vortex that torments you day in and day out. Unfortunately, such negative acquaintances are not the exception. They are the rule, and they are out there, waiting to cling to you for help. You can call them whenever you feel like it. There are energy vampires, narcissists, incompetent and envious people in society, eager to feed on your misery.

How can you tell if someone matches the characteristics of a negative person? Well, you can tell from the way you feel when you are around them. As mentioned earlier, these people aim at getting your precious energy and leaving you out to dry. They do not care about you, as you are simply a means for them to achieve what they want in life. You will notice that they will only seek your presence when they have something to take out of this interaction. Otherwise, a whole year may pass by without them calling or reaching out to you.

Negative people always use drama to get their way. They overreact and seek attention by putting themselves in the spotlight. You will see them crying and shouting, pitying themselves, and making others feel sorry for them. Don't fall into that trap. They are indeed miserable, but there is nothing you can do to help them. Unless they realize that they have a serious problem, you cannot possibly help them see the truth and change their behavioral patterns. It is more likely that you will be influenced by them, losing all your shine and feeling awful.

What you need to understand is that you are unique. You are magnificent, and you deserve to be loved and appreciated. Everyone around you should be able to see that and act accordingly. If they don't, they are not entitled to your time or interest. To that end, you should not chase people. Be yourself, and the right people will come to you. These are the persons that belong in your life, and they will be here to stay. If you notice a red flag, don't stick around to see where it leads you. It is highly likely that the person before you is going to let you down again and again. Make sure that you receive the respect you deserve rather than wonder if you are to blame in a relationship.

Learn how to set healthy boundaries that will keep you happy and prevent any bad blood along the way. In a relationship, you need to feel safe and secure about the person you have chosen by your side. You should love and care for them, expecting them to do the same. If you are always tending to their needs without getting anything in return, you must reassess your relationship and pursue something that truly lives up to your expectations. Needy people will be persistent and create a codependent environment, where they ask and you give nonstop. Get out of this vicious cycle, as it is going to eat you up and exhaust you before you know it.

Do not settle for less than what you have been dreaming about in your personal life. There is no point in being with someone who does not appreciate you for who you are. You don't need to be afraid of being alone. Being alone is much better than being stuck in an unhealthy, toxic relationship. Have an honest discussion and see where this is heading, based on your partner's answers. This doesn't mean that you should not fight for your relationship. Yet, when you do all the fighting, and they come off as indifferent, hostile, or manipulative, you really need to walk out and never look back.

Similar situations might arise at the office. It is great to cultivate an environment that celebrates teamwork and good ethics. Nevertheless, you should set healthy boundaries and prevent others from invading your private space. You need to be clear as to the relationships you are willing to form in your work environment. Again, just like in your personal life, you should under no circumstances accept being emotionally manipulated. There is no reason to fall for any blackmail, no matter how subtle or sophisticated it might be.

In the office, there are those who feed on other people's success and those who intimidate their colleagues in order to come across as leaders. These are, of course, just a few examples of personalities found in a workplace. Analyze the behaviors of your colleagues and associates. See through them and read their intentions. If you notice anything strange, confront them and let them know that you are not to be toyed with. Be the leader you have always wanted to be. Show off your leadership skills and be bold.

Clear out Your Emotional Baggage

It is of paramount importance for you to conserve energy for your self-actualization, awakening, and achievement of your dreams and goals. In your life, you simply don't have time to keep carrying around this baggage—if you are determined to live your dream. Find what is holding you back and make it go away. It's as simple as that. Sometimes it can be hard to define the root cause of our problem. We tend to overanalyze things and get caught up in misconceptions. However, you really need to dedicate the time and energy to discover your emotional baggage. As soon as you do, you should get ready to say "goodbye" to all your burdens from the past.

Imagine you are about to board a flight to your dream destination. You have checked in after planning your entire journey to this wonderful landscape. Suddenly, you feel something pulling you down. As you look down, you see a prisoner's ball and chain attached to your leg. What are you willing to do? Is this obstacle going to keep you from boarding the plane, or do you have what it takes to break off the chain? Although it is unlikely that you get into such a conundrum in real life, your emotional health can be jeopardized by such barriers.

EFT tapping can help you reprogram your brain so that you overcome the obstacles and continue on your path towards self-awareness and self-actualization. You can use this technique to repeat positive affirmations about yourself and your worth. If you want to get rid of the emotional discomfort associated with past experiences, rationalize them in a way that makes sense. Are you afraid of being incompetent of loving and being loved? Are you scared that you will end up alone and forgotten by everyone else? What you need is validation.

Make yourself heard. Talk loud and clear as you are tapping on your face and body. Repeat that you are worthy of love and compassion. You are a unique human being, showered with endless blessings in life. Say that you are loved and that there are people in your life acknowledging who you really are. You can modify your words according to your specific needs and desires. However, it is important that you remain honest. Repeat those words until you believe them as the indisputable truth. Never doubt yourself as to your true value.

EMOTIONAL INTELLIGENCE, SELF-AWARENESS, AND BALANCING EMOTIONS

Emotional intelligence has been associated with a negative connotation. The reason for that is its clear reference to being "emotional." This brings memories of intense outbursts, such as anger lashes and heavy crying. A person in a panic that cannot stop crying is described as being emotional. However, being emotional does not necessarily mean that you have emotional intelligence. The former is related to the fact that people express their feelings freely and without any hesitation. On the contrary, the latter has to do with acknowledging these emotions and knowing why you experience them.

In order to develop your emotional intelligence, you need to identify its basic components. First of all, this has to do with emotional awareness, which is empathy towards your own feelings and those of others. Then, emotional intelligence has to do with the ability to harness emotions and use them in problem-solving or thinking. Finally, it also includes the ability to handle emotions, being able to calm down yourself and others, or cheer up when it is required.

When you do not learn how to deal with emotions, you get to a point where you put the blame on yourself and think that everything you are doing is wrong. Other forms of lacking emotional intelligence include bullying others and being overly aggressive with them. This clearly stems from the inability to understand emotions and connect with others on an emotional level. But how can you develop such a social skill, which is crucial for your own happiness and for the entire society as well?

The answer lies in consciously working towards learning a new skill. If you want to be emotionally intelligent, you need to admit that you currently lack that. Through constant conscious efforts, you will get to the point where you apply your skill unconsciously, without even realizing it. There are several parts of improving this skill, which you ought to adhere to for optimal results. First of all, you should acknowledge your emotions. Differentiate and analyze them so that you are ready to accept and appreciate them. Reflect on emotions and where they stem from. Manage them, and finally, manage the emotions of others.

By working on self-awareness, you will get a ripple effect in almost everything in your life. It will help you understand your life so far and enable you to improve what you think is not working for you. In order to chart a course to your end destination, you must first identify where you are currently at. Know who you are as the first step in your effort to reach that higher purpose and spiritual growth in your life. This will allow you to become emotionally intelligent too.

In order to become more self-aware, you should never underestimate the power of journaling. As mentioned earlier, keeping a journal can be both eye-opening and liberating. It will create a safe ground to communicate with your inner self in an honest, productive manner. One simple exercise you can do is to start your day by writing three things that are bothering you and three things that you are grateful for. You can also do that before going to sleep.

After a whole week, check out those thoughts you have written down and identify the patterns that have started to form. After a month, you will see them more clearly. If you see that hanging out with a colleague makes you feel frustrated, then it is high time you stopped. Once you notice that coffee in the afternoon leads to agitated sleep, you should quit that habit and replace it with something else. As long as you are consistent with journaling, it is going to help you discover more about yourself.

As for the benefits you get out of journaling, you should not be surprised to know that it may lead to a decrease in anxiety, stress, and depression. At times, journaling can be as effective as cognitive behavioral therapy (psychotherapeutic treatment that aims at modifying negative behavioral patterns). Furthermore, journaling can be described as a form of meditation. You get to slow down and focus on a single thing. In that aspect, through journaling, you can control your emotions and boost self-awareness, as well as enhance your memory skills. When moving to physical manifestations, keeping a journal can result in an improved immune system and faster healing properties.

THE ART OF ANALYZING YOURSELF

Where do your emotions come from? Have you ever really wondered why you feel that way? If you want to become more self-aware, you need to analyze your feelings and try to reason with them. Of course, the way you feel has been formed throughout the years. Ever since your early childhood, your family has affected you greatly. In many cases, you have been forced to take on responsibilities that you should not have had to. However, these early experiences have shaped who you are right now.

An emotional shock absorber is a person who seeks codependent individuals to help. This is the only way they can be validated emotionally—through the process of helping others. Although this might sound selfless at first, it really stems from insecurity and the need to experience approval. Therefore, once you have identified such a pattern, it is best to deal with it and modify your behavior accordingly. Look after yourself so that you are able to give generously from a place of abundance instead of trying to give from a place that is drying out.

Once you know how you are feeling, you can take responsibility and face the world with respect and dignity. Otherwise, you will blame yourself for everything. Self-harming thinking is not the right way to go. Visualize the way you feel and project the way you want to feel. It is in your hands to shape new behavioral patterns that are healthier and more beneficial to you.

As energy centers, chakras are the doorways between your mental, your physical, and emotional bodies. You must balance those chakras and open them up, helping you with your emotions. In order to do so, you need to start from the base of your spine and the root chakra, imagining the color red and repeating the affirmation, *"I am grounded and supported."* Moving upwards, you balance your sacral chakra by imagining the color orange and repeating, *"I am connected and creative."* Solar plexus yellow-colored chakra can be balanced with the affirmation, *"I am united with the power of the universe."*

Heart chakra requires you to imagine the color green while repeating the affirmation, *"I give and receive unconditional love."* Throat chakra is blue-colored, and you can balance it by repeating, *"I speak my truth clearly and kindly."* Next, there is the third-eye chakra in indigo blue color. As our mind center, this is extremely important, and you can balance it by using the following affirmation, *"I am open to divine wisdom."* Finally, the violet-colored crown chakra can be balanced with the affirmation, *"I am one with the infinite all."* After doing that, you will feel any negative energy released, along with any blockages preventing you from expressing your true emotions.

Sometimes in life, we are trapped in a vicious cycle. There are emotional triggers that define the way we feel. Have you ever been sucked in a toxic relationship where the person sitting right in front of you was able to manipulate you in a heartbeat? This happens more often than you might imagine. People know which buttons to press, and we dance to their beat in return. Nevertheless, you are not powerless. You can change that, as long as you try.

First, you need to know where your wounds are. It seems that our feelings are directly linked to past experiences. If you have a wound from the past that has not healed properly, then your current behavior is a reflection of that wound. You then need to identify how you feel about the trigger. How does that make you feel? Analyze your emotions in an objective manner that allows you to see more clearly.

After that, it is time to change the story. Sometimes, triggers merely resemble our past wounds. It can be a great strategy to switch your perspective and give the other person the benefit of the doubt. This doesn't justify the bad behavior that has led to this trigger, but it allows you to get rid of any negativity. Once you take your own self out of the situation, you might be surprised by the explanations you can give. For instance, you can see that the other person is under a great deal of stress. There are moments in life where empathy can be amazingly helpful. Remember that relationships should not be seen as a reflection of your self-worth.

How to Read Others

When you are meeting someone for the first time, you are bombarded by a wealth of information. If you are able to process that information properly, then you will have the opportunity to read others like an open book. Even though many would say that verbal communication is the only thing you need to understand the intentions of your interlocutor, the truth is quite different. You figure out what the other person is all about through the interpretation of body language, the tone of their voice, and the words they use.

Let's begin with eye contact. In a romantic relationship, those in love will not be able to keep their eyes off each other. When you try to establish eye contact and the other person avoids it, then there is something wrong. If you are talking to someone and you notice that they are not blinking, this can be an indication that they are lying.

Next, watch a person's eyebrows. When they are raised, the person is either afraid, surprised, or worried. In any other event, the person who is raising their eyebrows is feeling uncomfortable.

When someone is smiling genuinely, there will be crinkles around the eyes. Otherwise, something is up. They might have a fake smile on their face, but you should be warned about it. Of course, you should pay attention to verbal communication. If a person is overly critical of a specific behavior, there is always the chance they are trying to mask their own behavior. Monotone replies usually mean that the person is not interested in what you are saying. When they use sarcasm, they actually mean the opposite of what they are saying to you. Check the emphasis they give so as to reveal their intentions.

If someone is interested in you and what you are saying, they will look you in the eye, and their body will face towards you as well. Frequently glancing elsewhere means that they are unconsciously trying to find an escape. Even though nodding tends to reveal agreement, when it is excessive, it might be a sign of anxiety or nervousness. The same happens when people constantly check their phones or their watch.

When a person is rubbing their chin, they are usually in the process of making a decision. On the other hand, a clenched jaw is an indication of stress and discomfort. Posture always reveals a lot about a person's character. When they are walking upright with their shoulders wide open, they are extremely confident. If they are slouching over and looking downwards as they speak, they are most likely self-conscious and lacking self-esteem. Rubbing your hands together generally means that you feel good about something.

Take a look at someone's shoes to get a better idea of who they are. If you see extremely clean shoes, then the person is nervous. Practical shoes are chosen by amiable people, and calmer types will usually wear uncomfortable shoes. Aggressive ones will select ankle boots. As for clothes, a detail-oriented person will be neat and smart in their outfit. A more casual wardrobe either reveals a creative soul or a messy person. When a person is untidy or gives off a bad smell, you should consider the possibility of them being lazy.

Make a special note of handshakes. A soft handshake might reveal someone submissive, whereas a handshake that is too hard typically means that the person is dominant. When the handshake is too long, it comes off as weird, while too short can indicate some sort of conflict. Now, as you may already know, crossed arms and legs represent physical barriers set by the person you are talking to. Last but not least, check out if the person you are speaking to is mimicking your body language. This is a clear sign that things are going well in your conversation.

Improving Emotional Intelligence at Home

Besides keeping a journal, here's a list of what you can do at home to improve your emotional intelligence:

- Be an active listener: In order to boost emotional intelligence, you need to listen and properly understand others. This will save you from a lot of heartbreak over the years.
- Do a self-evaluation: There are tests and quizzes available for you to take so that you identify any red flags and try to correct them.
- Put yourself in other people's shoes: This mental process will allow you to see things from a new, different perspective. Imagine you are someone else. What do you feel about a specific situation?
- Apologize: When you realize that you have made a mistake, apologize. Do not be selfish or shy away from this procedure. Say you are sorry, and do your best to avoid any similar events in the future.
- Stay positive: Throughout the day, focus on the positive

things in life. Express gratitude for all your blessings, and think of how to improve your own presence in the world.
- Observe: Observation is a key element of self-growth. Notice the way you talk to others and how you behave to them. In this way, you will be able to address your weak points.
- Listen to critique: When others tell you what they think of you, do not get offended. This is not the time for confrontation, rather for introspection. By fully comprehending who you are, you can reach self-awareness and unfold all those great things in life.
- Educate yourself: Listen to your mentors and experts who have perfected emotional intelligence. Find out what they do, how they behave in their everyday lives, and how they cope with the challenges ahead.
- Forgive: Don't hold grudges as they tend to poison you from within. Instead, try to let go and practice forgiveness. You will feel like a huge burden has been lifted off your shoulders.
- Get outdoors: Finally, be closer to nature. This will enable you to connect to the world and experience spiritual growth to get aligned with your emotions. In fact, observe nature all around you. Go for a walk, play with puppies or kittens, go mountain biking, or have a picnic under the graceful sunlight.

6

THE BEAUTY OF MISTAKES AND HOW SCREW-UPS CAN BOOST YOUR SELF-ESTEEM INTO THE STRATOSPHERE

Who can claim that they have never screwed up in their life? Not even once? I am guessing that number increases dramatically once we get the chance to see clearly who we are. Self-awareness comes with the acceptance that we are imperfect. This means we will make mistakes, one way or another. No matter how hard we try to succeed and do everything right, life gets in the way. We trust people that we shouldn't, we take risks that do not pay off, and the list goes on. After all, if things were that easy, would we get so much joy when accomplishing something great?

Avoiding mistakes is a good rule of thumb, but is that enough? Since you know you are going to screw up sooner or later, why torment yourself for something that was bound to happen either way? In fact, you can take these negative situations and so-called "failures" and use them to your own advantage. Reframing past experiences in a positive light for healing is a wonderful way to promote self-growth. You simply need to find the silver lining to reframe mistakes, failures, and painful memories, benefiting from the entire experience. Before you know it, you will turn them into victories and valuable lessons.

You can transmute negative memories into a positive future. There are several methods allowing you to do so, through visualization and other techniques like meditation, EFT tapping, and hypnosis. Learn how to reframe criticism and use other people's criticism as a wonderful gift. This will give you a great boost for the future. It will allow you to grow after having dealt with these issues that raise conflicts. There are always controversial personality traits, which you may not even realize. Unless you have really immersed in your unconscious mind, it is highly likely that you ignore several aspects of yourself. Do not think of criticism as something that offends your ego. If anything, it is an opportunity for you to improve yourself.

If you opt for self-awareness, you need to be surrounded by likeminded people that share the same interests as you. It is essential that you get inspired by people who have already accomplished their goals, having discovered their true calling and their higher purpose in life. These people will act as great role models, pushing you forward and bringing you closer to your goals. Rather than surrounding yourself with people who will stall or distract you from your end destination, it is crucial that you find a source of inspiration that fuels you even more.

It is therefore of paramount importance to seek help and guidance from those individuals who are able to pave the way, shedding light to the mysteries in life that might lead you astray. There are people who have mastered the art of self-actualization and they will assist you in your journey. They are the ones who will elevate your vibrational frequency, allowing you to attract all those blessings you wish to receive in life. Above anything else, though, these people will motivate you to establish a healthy and positive inner dialogue.

A HEALTHY AND POSITIVE INNER DIALOGUE

It is important that you maintain a healthy and positive inner dialogue. In fact, you should get so good at this that not even one depressing or negative thought pops in your mind. This can be achieved through hard and consistent work. You can practice and use exercises like yoga, meditation, journaling, EFT tapping, and much more.

I would suggest that you write a love letter to yourself. We could all use some more love in our lives. We are constantly in a hurry, rushing to complete all our tasks for the day. Yet, we don't get a moment to breathe and contemplate on how we treat ourselves. This is why it is of the essence to sit down, get rid of the tension, and focus solely on us. What do you need to hear today? What would you like someone else to tell you right now? This should be your compass as to what to include within your love letter.

Don't be shy since you are writing this letter to yourself. It doesn't have to be well-written, grammatically sound, and perfectly structured. What you need is the flow of emotions. Take a moment and think about what you are craving at this very moment. Is it encouragement? A pat on your shoulder? A reward for taking positive action, completing a project, or achieving a goal? Maybe it is all about validation that you are looking for. Imperfection and mistakes are the only way to grow. You must mess up to move forward in life, so don't get discouraged and write about these things.

This is your time. Lay back on that comfortable sofa, make yourself some herbal tea, and sit in silence. Get a lovely notebook and start writing something like this:

"Dear X, I am writing this letter to you right now because I feel that you are entitled to love. You are amazing. You are so thoughtful, caring, and understanding. Although you have a lot of stress in your life due to all the things you have taken on, you manage to pull through with a smile. Nothing gets you down, and you always know what to say to comfort others. I believe you are a person filled with love, compassion, and affection. I am so proud of you for having accomplished so much, despite all the obstacles that have tried to hinder your growth. You are a unique woman, blessed with beauty and creativity. I love you for who you are, and I wish you all the best in life. Stay strong, stay inspired, and keep on spreading the love in your life, inspiring others to do the same."

Of course, you can adjust the letter to your own personality and your special needs at the moment you are writing it. Be honest and generous with yourself. Let it be the beginning of continuous self-love you show to yourself, no matter how hard each day might be.

Trust Yourself

One of the basic concepts for you to work on should be your confidence. If you don't believe in yourself, who will? It is what you are projecting to the world. If you come across as self-conscious and always question your decisions, you automatically place others in the same situation. I know it can be hard to build your self-esteem overnight, and things don't work that way. However, you need to make a choice. Choose to be confident, not in the sense of being pompous or narcissistic. It is a form of protection.

Confidence is a choice, just as discipline and all of your circumstances are choices. Some choices are harder to make than others. Still, they define you and shape who you are in the world. Self-actualization plays a huge role in this process. By learning who you really are, you can skyrocket your self-esteem and achieve your goals, while clearing out any negative emotions that stop you from reaching the highest states of self-awareness. Of course, you need to plan ahead and organize your behavior in a way that welcomes progress. Take baby steps and walk one step at a time.

It is important to remember that you must always be yourself.

Don't pretend to be someone you are not, as the truth will set you free. Don't be afraid of making mistakes. Be true to yourself and take risks. Do what makes you happy, and you will be amazed at the results. People spend way too much time conforming to what rules dictate, trying to please others rather than sparking joy into their own life. You don't deserve that. Reveal your true self, and you will feel liberated from all the negative emotions that have been dragging you down.

Trust yourself to be good enough. If you fear anxiety, you shouldn't. This is your body's response to a potential threat. It should be like that, as this is the way you have been designed to act. However, you need to get out of your comfort zone. Being comfortable will only get you to a certain place. In case you want to get past that and achieve greatness, you should remove yourself from familiarity and convenience. Don't wait until you are ready. This will only increase the fear within you. Start with the easiest tasks and go for it.

Over time, you will build the capacity in yourself to do things you are uncomfortable with. You can train trust. Get out of your comfort zone and you will see that your self-esteem skyrockets right away. Even if at first you might feel awkward about doing something out of the ordinary, the outcome is going to compensate you fully for your boldness. After accomplishing the goals you have set, you will feel great about yourself and your ability to lead. Don't listen to everyone else. If someone doesn't recognize your worth, then that is on them. You cannot apologize for your choices, nor can you be a people-pleaser all the time. This is not your end goal in life, specifically when it comes to work-related matters.

Finally, make sure that you maintain healthy interests outside of work. This is the best way for you to become a wonderful leader. It is great to be committed to your work, but this doesn't mean that your life stops there. On the contrary, you should find the perfect balance between your personal and professional life. Spend time with loved ones, take on hobbies and activities that make you feel whole, take care of yourself, and have fun. When you do, you will realize that you perform even better at work. This happens because these parts of your life are interconnected and each of them affects the other.

7

SELF-COMPASSION, SELF-LOVE, AND SELF-FORGIVENESS

Self-love is all about how you take care of yourself on all different levels: physically, spiritually, mentally, and emotionally. You need to figure out how you treat yourself so that you are able to skyrocket your self-growth. Unless you learn how to love and care for yourself, you can never reach the highest levels of awareness and enjoy life to its fullest potential.

Unfortunately, sometimes you neglect yourself in your attempt to get things done within your busy day. You forget to eat, you never take a break, or even a moment to breathe. As a result, you end up feeling exhausted. This is not the way things are supposed to be. In fact, you must set your priorities straight and put yourself at the top. Only then can you gain a great perspective of your life and aim to the sky.

Do you love yourself? This is an awkward question, to be honest. The evident answer that comes to mind is that we all love ourselves. But is this true? There are several characteristics that will help you understand where you stand right now as far as self-love and self-compassion are concerned. First of all, are you grateful for what you have achieved so far in your journey? I am going to discuss gratitude below as a separate section of this chapter. Generally speaking, being grateful is a wonderful way of showing that you love and honor yourself.

Another key element of self-love is the ability to filter your thoughts and only attach to those that help you grow. If you take a moment and pay attention to what is going on inside your mind, you will notice hundreds of different thoughts. Fears and insecurities, anxiety and stress, thoughts that interpret your emotions, and positive and negative manifestations are all there. If you choose to attach to every single thought of yours, you will end up going crazy or being paralyzed by their vastness and intensity. What you need to do is pick just the thoughts that light up your day and focus on them.

Moving forward, here is a no-brainer. If you love yourself, then you need to forget all about perfectionism. You don't need to excel at everything. Obviously, it is great to master the skills that are relevant to your higher calling in life. Yet, it is not necessary or even expected of you to be great at every single thing you do. If you focus on your inner critic, you will only bruise your ego and get nothing in return. Avoid criticism and be compassionate with yourself. It is good to aim at self-improvement and growth, as long as any lack in performance is not deemed as a failure.

Equally important is the physical care of your body. Although most people would take it for granted, the truth is that not everyone can take pride in how they treat their physical presence. In this chaotic world, it can be hard to lead a healthy lifestyle. There are so many distractions out there, as well as obligations that consume a lot of your time and drain you of the energy to be good to yourself. Nonetheless, you must find the time and the energy to dedicate to your body. Choose the right foods over junk food. Eat wholesome vegetables and fruits, seasonal and organic when possible. Limit your sugar and flour intake, avoid processed and artificial foods, and drink a lot of water.

I am pretty sure you already know this, but it is essential to remain active and fit. Select a type of exercise that best matches your personality, easing yourself into it. You might love hitting the gym or walking daily. Jogging, swimming, mountain biking, or yoga sessions are all exceptional forms of exercise. Be consistent with your workout routine so that you get the optimal results. Apart from shedding any excess weight, exercise is great for your heart and overall health. It also enables you to release stress and any negative energy that has remained stagnant for long.

Besides all of the aforementioned properties, self-love is directly linked to the quality of your self-talk. Have you ever realized how harsh you can be with yourself? When you are talking to yourself, are you filtering anything? Unfortunately, most of us are judgmental towards ourselves and end up accusing ourselves for all the bad things that are going on in our life. Imagine trying to run a marathon even though you have never done that before. You have trained enough, and your stamina has improved dramatically. You feel self-confident, and then someone starts calling you names, criticizing you every step of the way. How can you expect to make it to the finish line?

The next thing I am going to talk about is stepping out of your comfort zone. This might baffle you a little as to why it has its place among self-love practices and habits. Well, if you think about it, you will see why I have included it here. When you take a step further out of your comfort zone, you immediately become vulnerable. However, at the same time, you also open up to new experiences. Why would you ever want to settle for things in life you have already experienced when there is still so much out there for you to discover? By making eye contact or talking to a complete stranger, participating in environmental projects with people you don't know, or bungee jumping from the edge of a steep cliff, you open yourself to new adventures, new feelings, and endless possibilities.

I cannot stress enough the importance of avoiding comparing yourself to other people. This is the epitome of self-love because it can easily lead to a slippery slope for you. Self-love is all about accepting and loving yourself unconditionally. When you attempt to compare yourself to others, you instantly forget about this fundamental truth, and you get into some sort of contest. What is more, you indirectly admit that you are not good enough. If you are looking somewhere else to validate your worth, then it is clear that you do not believe in yourself like you should. You put yourself in a position where you must account for your current status, and this is really horrible. It is of the essence that you recognize you are a unique being. By default, you cannot be compared to anyone else in the world.

Now let's focus on self-forgiveness. Everything is a co-creation, so anything you feel guilty about isn't necessarily all your fault. You must forgive yourself and let guilt go if you are determined to reach your full potential. It is crucial that you forgive yourself, as well as others. You cannot reach the highest levels of self-awareness unless you have settled any grudges you may hold or feelings of guilt and shame. No one is perfect in this life. We all make mistakes, and it is only natural that you experience such negative feelings sometimes in your life.

Forgiveness is a true virtue. It reveals the greatness of the person who forgives, letting the world know that they do not wish to charge their life negatively and sabotage any effort of theirs to ascend to a higher ground. By learning how to forgive yourself, you become a better person. Of course, forgiveness cannot be seen as a justification for any malicious intent. This doesn't give you the right to harm yourself or others. It doesn't give you the right to engage in illegal activities or lead a life that is not blessed with love, compassion, and justice. Some people might argue that self-forgiveness is just an alibi for any wrongdoing. This could not be any further from the truth. By letting go of negative feelings such as guilt and shame, you show how much you love yourself, and you offer a way out of never-ending torment.

Finally, self-love is closely related to self-exploration in terms of feelings, emotions, and habits. You need to identify your true purpose in life or else discover your dharma. Even though you may not have found it yet, you must constantly explore yourself to find what truly makes your soul sing. When you do, it will all start making sense. Your life is going to gain a brand new meaning. You will no longer drift away from your focus since you will have realized what you are meant to do in this world. Discovering that higher purpose is the most eloquent proof of self-love.

After having analyzed the basic features of self-love, do you think you practice that enough in your everyday life? I am guessing you wish you gave more love and attention to yourself. Below you will find some really simple and easy exercises to do at home in order to boost that feeling of self-compassion and care about yourself. They are based on the principles of EFT tapping, and you can repeat them as often as you like.

EASY-TO-FOLLOW EXERCISES

It is all about boosting your self-love. According to what you seek in life, there are special affirmations for you to use towards enhancing self-love, self-compassion, and self-forgiveness. One of the best methods, as described earlier, is through EFT tapping. Just make sure that you follow a specific rhythm while tapping the different parts of your face and body, and repeat the EFT tapping guide for three whole rounds.

As we learned about EFT in Chapter 4, there are affirmations that enhance the whole process. I have included a list with the most inspiring things to say during your EFT tapping session. You will see that I have divided them into two groups, depending on what you chose to focus on each time. Obviously, you can modify them as per your own needs and preferences. Furthermore, you can even combine affirmations from both the lists for a holistic approach to your self-awareness ritual.

The affirmations that can be used for self-love and self-compassion are the following:

- I love and accept myself completely and unconditionally.
- I am beautiful, both inside and out.
- My opinion matters.
- I am intelligent, and I inspire others with my knowledge.
- I have the power to change.
- I love myself even with my flaws and insecurities.
- I deserve to be happy in life.
- Love flows from within me.
- I let go of negative self-talk and concentrate on positive things.
- I am capable of reaching my goals.
- I love and accept all of me.
- My capacity for love is infinite.
- I allow myself to feel deeply and love without any condition.
- I love my body, as this is what I was born with.
- It is in my power to achieve anything I set my mind to.
- I experience constant growth every single day.
- I have a warm and caring heart.
- I am able to overcome any challenge with grace and dignity.
- I believe in myself.
- I love every part of who I am, because every part of me defines me.

The affirmations that can be used for self-forgiveness are the following:

- I forgive myself.
- I release the heavy burden of self-hatred, guilt, and shame.
- I am at peace with myself.
- I will treat myself with respect and kindness from today forward.

- I exchange my shame and anger for self-love and self-compassion.
- I forgive those who have wronged me, and I choose to live a life full of love, joy, and peace.
- I step away from any resentment I had in the past.
- The past holds no power over me, and therefore I am in control of forgiving myself and others who have wronged me.
- I am willing to overcome my limitations and forgive myself completely.
- My happiness is more important to me than any urge to hold grudges.
- As I change my thoughts and let go of anger, guilt, and shame, the world around me changes too.
- I am letting go, and I am ready to move forward with my life.
- I take full responsibility for my actions, and I forgive myself wholeheartedly.
- My spiritual development allows me to forgive myself and others.
- I forgive myself for being imperfect, as we are all humans, and nobody in this life is perfect.
- Each day is a new opportunity. As I seize the day and get ready to benefit from these new opportunities waiting ahead for me, I choose to forgive myself.
- I choose to forgive myself and everyone else in the past, and I choose to love myself into the future.
- I am a forgiving, loving, gentle, and caring human being.
- The past is gone, and I live in the present moment. Therefore, I forgive myself and all others for anything that has happened in the past.

Gratitude and Dealing with Inner Conflicts
One of the major components of self-love is gratitude. If you

want to experience the magnitude of life and its beauty, you should not be in a state of lacking things. Of course, there will always be room for improvement. Many people will always be richer or poorer than you. They will be taller or shorter, more successful, and so on. It is up to you to decide how to look at things in life. You can choose to nag all the time because you have not yet achieved your goals. You can choose to be jealous of others who have managed to accomplish their own goals sooner than yourself. But how would that make you feel?

You must realize that you have been blessed in life. Therefore, you should give "thanks" to the world for everything you have received so far. This opens up your being to a receiving mode, which in turn attracts even more wonderful things your way. Obviously, you will always want to experience more successes in your life, and this is completely understandable. However, you need to remain grounded and be satisfied with what you have right now. Enjoy where you are, what you have achieved up to this very moment, and feel content about that.

GRATITUDE RADIATES THAT POSITIVE, GLOWING ENERGY WITHIN you. It is such a powerful thing to practice so that you are happy in your life every single moment. More than that, gratitude reveals a deep self-love. You don't put too much pressure on yourself to accomplish all the goals that you have set in the first place. Instead, you reward your persistence and dedication to your journey, and you have a great time. This is what you should be thinking of, no matter the obstacles that always get in the way and distract you from reaching your end goal.

When was the last time you expressed your gratitude for the things that you have accomplished in life? When did you think about all the great things you have received in your journey towards enlightenment, self-growth, and development? It is important that you do that daily. In this way, you will never distract your mind or get carried away by false expectations and unrealistic goals. It is of the essence to stay connected to your true self and really take in the joy and satisfaction deriving from these blessings of yours.

There will be times when progress is slow. Although you might be eager to succeed in life right away, it is not always possible to do so. A million things can get in the way and stall your progress. This doesn't mean that you should feel deprived of whatever you have achieved so far. On the contrary, it should make you even more determined to try harder towards accomplishing your goals. Find the extra motivation you need so that you notice the silver lining even in the worst-case scenario. Don't anticipate change, but instead be patient, and let those wonders unfold before your eyes when you least expect them.

Create a morning ritual that supercharges your self-awareness and ensures that you are happy in your life. Take just 5 minutes in the morning and just smile. At first, you might feel uncomfortable smiling without anyone noticing. Over time, you will do it subconsciously and love to watch your smiling reflection in the mirror. There is no right way of doing that. You just start smiling and focus on this act of yours. If you like, you can look in the mirror. Otherwise, just sit there, smile, and think happy thoughts.

Next, take a moment and state 10 things you are grateful for. Do you find the number too high? Luckily for you, there are many more blessings in your life, and I am sure of it. For instance, you can say something like:

- I am healthy.
- I am happy in my life.
- I am successful and accomplished.
- I am compassionate.
- The people close to me love me unconditionally.
- I am insightful and inquisitive.
- I love my job.
- I have found my true calling in life.
- My family and I are all healthy and happy.
- I am grateful for my cute and loving pet.
- I am aligned with the universe.

By doing so, you will see that you have so many things to be happy about and brag about. Don't be afraid to admit that you have been blessed with these things. There is nothing wrong with speaking the truth. You are beautiful, you are amazing, and you are a good listener. You are intelligent and you have a wonderful family, caring friends, and a healthy working environment. The list goes on and on. No matter what you choose to include in your positive affirmations about the things you are grateful for, it will raise your vibration, and you will then attract more goodness into your life.

Now, let's focus on internal conflicts and how they can affect your life in more ways than you could ever have imagined. Have you ever been torn between two different and opposing needs that require your utmost attention? This is what an inner conflict looks like. For example, you are feeling lonely, and you wish to hang out with your friends. At the same time, you have an important deadline to adhere to. So, in this case, your inner conflict is torn between your need to experience companionship and your need to do your work and get paid for it. Similarly, you have only a limited amount of money at hand. You can either pay for the utility bills or pay the rent. Either way, you have to decide which necessity you value higher and go with that.

It is important to identify these inner conflicts, as they will most probably cause discomfort and anxiety to you. Since you cannot please both sides, you will end up feeling insecure about whether or not you have made the right decision. In the first example, by choosing to go out with your friends, you sabotage your work and probably mess with your finances. By choosing to stay at home and work on your project, you risk feeling so lonely that you simply cannot function. In the second example, you can either choose to pay rent and risk losing your phone connection or even electricity, or confront your landlord and possible eviction.

You cannot escape inner conflicts, as they are pretty much unavoidable. We live complex lives, meaning that sometimes our needs will overlap. Since we cannot control everything, we will have to prioritize and base our decisions on our own set of values. Not being able to actually resolve a problem can create a constant feeling of anxiety and stress. Chronic stress may lead to even more severe health conditions and deteriorate your quality of life. Unless you fully comprehend how inner conflicts work and unless you come to terms with your limited control over things, you will continue suffering from this emotional rollercoaster.

In order to deal with inner conflicts, it is essential that you analyze both sides. In this way, you become fully aware of the situation. By having more facts at hand, you will have the chance to make much more concrete decisions that help you minimize your stress. This can be hard to accomplish because sometimes there is a hidden part of an inner conflict, often attached to painful memories, that you have repressed in your unconscious mind. However hurtful this process might be, it is important that you go through it.

Then it is time for you to evaluate both sides and realize that every problem is indeed resolvable. After having spent enough time weighing the pros and cons of each side, you will be ready to make a sound and deliberate decision. Once you do that, you will see that you are left with a deep sense of calmness and safety. You have done everything within your power, and you are sure about your decision.

8

INNER COURAGE & SELF-RESPECT

Regrets really stem from a lack of courage. We tend to regret things we did or didn't do because we lacked the courage to pursue our desires. There are many reasons driving our lack of courage. Not being true to yourself may lead to regrets. Maybe we are afraid of the unknown. What will the consequences be? What will others think about me? To avoid fear, we settle for less than what we could have achieved. We confine ourselves in a smaller space, living our life of quiet desperation. But does that make us feel happy?

A disempowered person has given up the opportunity to fulfil the purpose of their life. Do you have the courage to let go of things that despise you in life? Fear of rejection often leaves you emotionally crippled, hiding behind a veil of mediocrity. It is that sense of vulnerability that prevents you from speaking your own, core truth. However, this is how you get to express your vital life force. By suppressing it, you essentially sabotage yourself from living to your full potential.

Choose to go beyond the comfort zone of the collective in order to grow into your own full potential. Do not limit yourself to the norm. Be courageous enough to extend further and accomplish better outcomes. This will be the beginning of your unfolding path towards a satisfying life. What about what others think of your behavior? Let go of external expectations and peer pressure. You should be bold and walk on your own path rather than follow in the footsteps of others.

Express yourself in a kind and compassionate way that creates space for healing. Don't be afraid of what others may think of you. Remember that we are all in a different place within our journey. Therefore, you should not judge others simply because they do not behave like you do. Distill your own truth, and let others follow their true path in life, whether or not it is aligned with yours. If you are determined to experience enrichment and joy in life, you must establish high-quality relationships.

Do not expect happiness to come to you externally, using self-imposed conditions. Happiness is a choice. It is a decision that flows from within you. When you honor the truth of your being, you find happiness. Your highest power and ultimate fulfillment derives from facing the fears that keep holding you back. Stretch your life so as to grow and expand. Take risks in the very same circumstances that make you feel uncomfortable.

Be humble and acknowledge the limitations in your life. Nobody can be perfect at everything. Unless you come to terms with that, you will never be satisfied. You will always anticipate more. Even if you achieve something wonderful, you will still be judgmental about yourself and the way you have acted. Humility is a virtue which helps you gain a true perspective of life. In this way, you will not criticize others, and you will not be too harsh on yourself.

Always express gratitude for your blessings. It takes courage to admit that you have been blessed with so many things in life. There is nothing wrong with being privileged. You should not feel ashamed about that, as you have not wronged anyone else. You deserve all the good things that come your way, and you should be grateful for receiving them. According to the Law of Attraction, this will allow you to become even more abundant and receive even more blessings in your life. Be open to them, expressing your content and appreciation.

There will be moments where you need to surrender to the course of life. Things cannot always go exactly as planned. Life is filled with challenges, and this is completely understandable. You need to accept things as they come and learn how to adapt to reality. Of course, this doesn't mean that you should give up or compromise with less than what you deserve. Nevertheless, a setback should not bring you down.

Love others as you love yourself. You are not alone in the universe. Altruism is among the finest principles in life, demonstrating concern for others and their happiness. It is your responsibility as a citizen of the world to make this world better. Charity is a great way for you to give back and care for those in need. It keeps you grounded and connects you to the rest of the world. Volunteer whenever you can so that you contribute to society. This will not only show the love you have for others, but also boost your self-respect.

Last but not least, you should have resilience and strength. No matter how hard the waves come your way, you need to be strong and willful to overcome them. Things will get hard, and you will be beaten off at times. Remember that there is always a rainbow waiting at the end of the heaviest storm. Be ready to withstand the storm so that you can enjoy the beauty of the rainbow. Build your defense in a way that prevents others from hurting you. Even when they do, stay focused on your goals, and take the punches as they come.

Implement all these qualities in your life so that you enhance your self-respect and become more courageous. Be bold, be brave, and learn how to reprogram your mind so that you achieve greatness through courage.

REPROGRAMMING YOURSELF

It is important that you implement mechanisms in your everyday life that allow you to feel confident and gain the courage it takes to live the life you deserve. Below, I have provided EFT affirmations that target this specific aspect and enable you to feel braver and more confident. Just think of something that is troubling you. Think of something that prevents you from moving forward in your life. Maybe it is something you feel you are not good at, or perhaps something that makes you feel embarrassed about yourself.

After having focused on the specific trigger, it is time to concentrate on your body. Where exactly do you feel the fear, the stress, or the anxiety? Scan your body from the top of your head all the way to your toes. Do you feel it in your chest, in your abdominal area, or in your head? Now that you have pinpointed where that feeling stems from, try to determine its intensity. On a scale of 1 to 10, how stressed are you? How afraid are you? This is going to help you in the healing process.

You should use the EFT tapping sequence that has been described in detail earlier in the book, while repeating the following affirmations that aim at shifting your mindset: *"Even though I am afraid to move forward, I love and accept myself. Although I don't think I am good enough, I love and accept myself completely. I am good enough, but I am afraid to do this. I am scared. I am worried. I don't know if I can do this right. My mind is troubled by this all the time. I am worried about what others think of me. I am afraid of being rejected and putting myself out there. Failure scares me. I am scared about not succeeding."*

Slowly but steadily, you now need to identify the fact that there are no grounds for your insecurity. You don't have to feel afraid, as the fear you are feeling does not get validated. In fact, reality proves you wrong. *"This fear and this worry is irrational. It doesn't make sense. Even if I know I can do this, there is still a part of me that is afraid. I don't know why I am afraid. I keep thinking of the worst-case scenarios that will play out, instead of the best ones."* Take a deep breath. Relax and think about the intensity of the very same feeling you had before this session. Has it remained the same or has it become lower?

After feeling comfortable with these affirmations, you should dig even deeper. *"Even though I am good at this, I am afraid that others will judge me. I am afraid that I am not good enough and that others will be disappointed in me. Although I have always performed well, I still don't feel confident. I wish I were someone else. I don't want others to see me as vulnerable. When I don't know something, I don't want others to see that I am still learning. I prefer being an expert. But I am human, so I am imperfect. I would like to give this a try, but I am still afraid. I would like not to be scared, but I am. I hope other people don't judge me, as I don't judge others."*

If you focus on the intensity of your feeling, it is most likely that it will have dropped a few points. It will now be a little easier for you to imagine doing what has been causing you so much stress and fear. Your energy will have shifted. Don't be alarmed if you feel the energy moving within your body. The final affirmations should be as follows: *"I would like to feel more confident. I know I can't be perfect because no one is perfect. Either way, I completely love and accept myself. I am feeling a little more confident right now. I don't know if I am ready to go out there and do what is making me feel scared, but I can do this. It is possible for me to do this. Maybe I am more courageous than I thought. I am brave. I have a lot of skills and talents. There are people who are less capable than me and those who are more capable than me. That's completely understandable. I would like to get out of my comfort zone. I can try it out, because I feel confident about myself. Yes, I am confident."*

Of course, you are free to modify the wording of this session as per your own personal needs. Hopefully, by the end of this session you will have dropped the intensity of your fear or anxiety a little further down. Even if you haven't, though, you should stick to this ritual. Your energy has been stuck and needs to move. Repeat the session every time you feel stressed so that you get instant relief and a boost of courage. This will help you reach your goals and become more courageous, dealing with the root of your fear.

Besides EFT, you can repeat positive affirmations for brave living. Be careful not to freeze your sympathetic nervous system by staying in "fight or flight" mode or being triggered too often. This can shut off your reproductive system, creativity, and lust for life. This can also affect your immune system. It is imperative that you clear out old emotional baggage and calm your nervous system if you wish to reach your full self-awareness potential. Courage can be trained, and therefore these affirmations will show you the way to believe in yourself. When you are about to question yourself, repeat the following:

- I am brave and bold in life.
- Great courage lies within me.
- Even though I feel fear, I move forward in my pursuit of greatness.
- I love and accept myself.
- I am ready to take action, regardless of my fear.
- I am courageous and confident in my life .
- Despite my discomfort, I am going to succeed.
- Fear doesn't define me.
- I am proud of myself for being brave and bold.
- I face every challenge in my life with courage.

Respect Who You Are and Self-Reflect
Self-respect means that you are proud of who you are, even if you have made mistakes in life. You look in the mirror and see your reflection, thinking that you love and accept yourself no matter

what. You are grateful for what you have achieved in life, even with the hardships and the failures that you have been through. When you respect yourself, you never compromise your well-being.

When you practice self-respect, you can take an honest look at yourself to move forward in the life direction that you want. Whatever hurts you only makes you stronger in life. Even if you have made mistakes, they can serve as lessons learned that contribute to your progress. In order for you to have self-esteem and self-respect, you don't need to be a millionaire or be the most intelligent person in the room. You don't have to be a successful businessman or own a fancy car to gain respect.

You are proud of who you are and of the person you have become. It takes courage to admit where you have been wrong, as well as acknowledge that the path has been rocky and steep. It takes courage to own your victories as much as your losses. Seeing yourself exposed like that, without any distorting lens, lets you observe clearly every single detail. This is going to hurt, but it is imperative that you face the truth. Only by doing so can you become self-aware and reach the spiritual growth you have been anticipating all this time.

Obviously, you are not going to like everything you see. There are things you might loathe about yourself—things that make you mad, like bad habits and feelings that you wish you didn't have. You know very well that nobody is flawless. Still, there are things that you would change in a heartbeat if you could. By respecting yourself, you take full responsibility, and you try to correct what is not doing you justice. To do that, you need to find a strategy that helps you reprogram your mind and reach that point where you free yourself of those limitations.

Even though you are a creature of habit, you can hack your brain and modify your behavior accordingly. It is possible to retrain your mind so that you get a reward out of the habits that are actually good for you. A key element to be successful in this process is your awareness. By being aware of the things you should change. You have taken the first step to modify them. Since you identify that something is bad for you, do whatever it takes to be the person you deserve to be. Towards achieving that shift, you need to update the reward value. This is called "reward-based learning," and it can help you break bad habits.

9

WHY ALL THE SELF-GROWTH? WHY FIND YOUR DHARMA? WHAT DO YOU REALLY WANT?

Do you know what you really want in life? Most humans float through life without any self-awareness or goals. They go through life without any meaning, wasting their precious time, and they don't even realize that. It is imperative that you find your true purpose in this lifetime to reach your full potential and become fulfilled. Otherwise, you will always feel that emptiness deep inside. There will be moments when you are going to feel saddened without actually being able to justify that emotion. You will feel incomplete.

It's not just success you are after but who you will become in the process. Of course, it is great to be the best in a specific field. It is amazing to excel at a job, a sport or any other endeavor. Nevertheless, this is not the only thing that should drive you towards mastering your skills. It is the feeling of accomplishment that you are after, becoming absolutely aware of who you are and what you are meant to do.

In a world filled with so many different paths, we often find ourselves wondering what we should decide. Is this decision going to define our entire existence from now on? This realization can become a huge burden falling on your chest and leaving you gasping for air. You should not be afraid of making decisions. In fact, this is the magic of being free and independent in this world. You should embrace it and welcome it with open arms.

Decision making has been associated with masculine thinking because it is based on logic and facts. Even though they are critical components of a firm, solid decision, you should never underestimate the great contribution of feminine thinking. What about your intuition and empathy? What about emotional intelligence and a sense of compassion? It is a blend of those characteristics that guarantee the optimal result for you and your future.

We are all scared of the consequences that a decision of ours might have in our life. However, we should not back down or appoint anyone else as a decision-maker. Remember that when you give in to fear, you give away your power, and you disconnect from who you really are and what you really want. There are actions and non-actions. You need to be responsible for both these aspects of your decision-making process. You must own them. Don't get carried away by the impulse to act always, even when inaction is the most suitable approach. Sometimes waiting creates a conscious type of patience, and this is absolutely fine.

Evaluate your circumstances and decide whether or not to act. Even if you make a mistake, it doesn't matter. What matters the most is to take charge of your life, rather than being a mere spectator of the events that unfold before your eyes. Listen to your inner self so that you find what you really want. Follow your dharma —your higher purpose in life. Once you have found what you are destined to do in this world, you will feel enlightened and accomplished. You will transform your everyday life in ways you have not even begun to imagine.

The first step should be to identify where exactly you have been holding yourself captive. Be honest with yourself and take an inquisitive look so as to observe and take all the information in. Don't be afraid to put yourself out there. Admit what you know that you wish you didn't know. It is of paramount importance to see the truth of who you are. Even if it is hurtful, you must go through the process of acceptance.

Follow your own truth and express yourself, regardless of how that makes others feel. It is your life, and you should be held accountable for any of your decisions. Choose to expand rather than contract and experience joy rather than fear. Choose excitement over dread and liberation over suffocation. Finally, engage with what you want. Steer clear of perfectionism and seek clarity through self-awareness.

I know that the road to self-awareness can be hard and long. What makes it even harder and longer, though, is procrastination. This has been one of the major issues of concern for people of all backgrounds. Artists, creative designers, architects, politicians, entrepreneurs, students, and teachers alike experience this avalanche that comes their way and stalls their progress. How can you avoid that?

DESTROY YOUR DISTRACTIONS

There are times in your life when you get filled with so many things to do. There are deadlines everywhere, slowly creeping in and distracting you from thinking clearly. How do you manage these distractions? Most people, if not all of us, experience the "monkey mind." This represents the unsettled and uncontrollable, whimsical, and fun side of life. Imagine you are always on vacation somewhere nice and sunny. Our brain has been programmed so as to pursue things that are fun and easy (Urban, 2013). There is nothing wrong with that, obviously. But what happens when we need to move past that?

Assuming that we spent our lives doing only the things that we found fun and easy, humankind would not be the same. People would not have been able to achieve great things since they would be busy gaming or chatting with friends. However, in our mind there is also a place for prudent decision-making. The problem is that those two entirely different aspects of ourselves need to work together. Instead of cooperating, sometimes they tend to antagonize themselves for our attention. This is where everything falls apart.

If you want to increase your self-awareness, you need to acknowledge that lovely monkey inside your head. Yet, you also need to know how to tame it. It is in your hands to move past distractions and procrastination. Although they are part of your being, you should find ways to overcome this barrier that has been making your life more hectic. Instead of delaying or postponing tasks, make sure that you divide them into more achievable chunks and stick to a routine. In this way, you will complete smaller milestones and adhere to your deadlines more easily.

Procrastination will keep you away from your highest purpose in life, and you don't want that. Even though you are getting temporary pleasure from what you are doing as a procrastinator, deep inside, you are tormented by feelings of self-guilt, disappointment, and lack of self-worth. You believe that it is your fault you cannot get things done, decreasing your value as a person. Such an attitude is totally different from what should be driving you in life. It will keep you numb and unable to ascend to the highest levels of self-awareness. Why would you do that to yourself?

People need to find their true calling—their vocation in life to follow. This is called dharma and reflects who you are meant to be in this world. The cosmos has been aligned in a way that enables you to pursue this higher calling, doing what you have always been meant to do (Saiisha, 2020). Once you find your dharma, it can lead to fulfillment and abundance. In that aspect, dharma is a blend of your natural inclinations and your duties in everyday life. It combines what you have been destined to do, along with what you need in order to get by and progress.

Have you found your true calling? If you are still wondering, then the answer is most probably "no." Yet, it lies within you. Search in your soul for the thing that lights a sparkle and makes you feel great. There are two key elements that will help you stay true to your dharma. Unify your life energy around it, devoting most of your day doing what you have been sent to do. You have been given a sacred gift, a talent, or an inclination in life. It is up to you to make the most of it and unfold its magical essence. You need to create the right conditions so that your dharma can flourish.

The second key element is to dedicate 10,000 hours of your time towards your dharma. If you want to achieve mastery in piano music, then you need to devote at least 10,000 hours learning how to play. Learn the theory, practice, get a variety of songs and melodies; do whatever makes you the best in what you do. World-class athletes, artists, and entrepreneurs dedicate a vast percentage of their day to acquire skills and perfect them. This is what makes them shine, and it is their own deliberate decision. Therefore, your entire life should revolve towards a focused concept of your mastery.

Take ownership of your thoughts and harness that energy for purposeful activity, instead of leaving it to a random or reactive response. Although the thought is not your choice, your reaction to it is. You must deliberately focus on your thoughts as a way to identify personal choices for decision-making. Evaluate the impact each decision has on your self-growth. Is your diet consistent with your goals? Are your sleeping patterns in line with your life's purpose? Are your dating patterns helping you reach your desired state, or are they sabotaging you?

It can be chaotic to put all these things into order. Even when you know where you are headed, it is difficult to manage everything. This is why you need a system. You need a tangible means of taking control over your goals. In this way, you will be able to evaluate your progress and modify things that might not work as planned. This is a dynamic process, which means that you can change the things that don't function properly and pick the ones that do. One of the methods for you to organize your tasks and keep things in order is through journaling.

Get a notebook and write down your spiritual, health, relationship, financial, and work-related goals. This will give you a clear vision of what you want to achieve in your life. In this way, you can reveal your dharma and make sure that you stay true to yourself. Refer to that notebook, adding things as you go. It will be a constant reminder of how far you have come and how far you want to be. Having a visual of your genuine calling will help you avoid distractions and procrastination.

Perseverance, Discipline, and Empowerment

Now that you are already in a state of inspiration, do some goal setting. Don't hold back any longer, and don't let this precious time pass you by. By procrastinating, you withhold yourself from what you truly deserve. Once you find your dharma, you will see that everything becomes clearer. You will not need to pressure yourself to dedicate more time in your endeavors as this will flow naturally. It is going to feel like all the pieces of your puzzle have finally been completed.

You must persevere. Stick to your goals, no matter how hard they may seem. Unless you put in some real effort, you cannot expect to reap the benefits of your self-growth. Being aware of the hardships does not take away any of the glory for you. Instead, it only adds to your accomplishments. Even if you are feeling exhausted or too tired to push forward and try harder, don't get carried away by the temporary content of procrastination. In the end, you will be rewarded by finding your life's purpose and laying the foundations for your own masterpiece.

Be disciplined so that you achieve your goals in a timely manner. Your life is invaluable, and you need to realize that right now. Focus on your goals and discipline yourself in order to maximize your potential. These goals need to include not only business or financial plans. They should also feature spiritual, self-awareness, charity, and dharma (purpose) goals. If you want to conquer the top, you must be ready to work hard and exceed your boundaries. Work compassionately but still maintain a rhythm that allows you to grow and create. This requires a lot of your time, energy, and resources. Offer that generously, as they will eventually reward you.

Finally, be empowered. Find the constant motivation to push forward. There are times when you would rather sit back and relax instead of giving your full attention to your goals. Don't give in to that impulse, as it will gradually eat you up and leave you hanging out to dry. Discover what keeps you going and use that to fuel your passion, your energy, and your determination. Empowerment is of the essence when it comes to dealing with long-term goals and mastering your skills. So find what ticks the boxes for you and refer to that ritual whenever you feel like you could use a boost.

10
AMAZING GUIDED MEDITATIONS TO SUPERCHARGE YOUR SELF-AWARENESS

By now, you already know why it is essential to boost self-awareness and know the real "you." Otherwise, you cannot unfold your true calling in life and experience absolute content in your every day. One of the best methods to know yourself and discover who you are destined to be is through meditation. By focusing on the present moment and getting rid of distractions, you connect with your spiritual self. This allows you to silence the background and concentrate solely on what matters.

Below, I have created four special guided meditations that will enable you to find yourself. They have been designed with the aim of helping you reach your goals. Whether you wish to align with the universe and remain grounded or you want to let go of past regrets and guilt, these meditations will take you by the hand and walk you through the entire process of self-actualization. Are you ready to supercharge your self-awareness?

GUIDED MEDITATION FOR SELF-REALIZATION

This meditation is an excellent way for you to calm your mind and get rid of your anxiety. It is a great option for re-aligning yourself with the universe, gaining a different perspective of life.

Sit somewhere quiet and close your eyes. Picture the surface of the sun. It is bright, illuminating the universe. In a corner, there is the earth that is floating. Imagine earth as a small black dot, moving slowly and at a fixed pace. Start visualizing all the problems you have in this world—all the chaos created in society and all the hatred and fear. All these negative feelings—the bad situations that you find yourself in—are happening right now in this small black dot. The things that are so important to us only represent a tiny part of the universe.

Only through self-realization can you understand what you are part of. By realizing where you are, who you are, and what role you play in the universe, you can perceive the world objectively and without any distortion. You comprehend that you are part of something much greater. You are so small, even though when bad things are happening, you think that the whole universe revolves around you.

Hover from the distance as if you are observing earth from space. Watch the earth as it is passing by the surface of the sun slowly, and gain perspective of the vastness of the universe. Everything you think you are is happening on that tiny ball you are watching move so slowly. Six billion other people are found on that black dot, looking like tiny organisms that are invisible to the naked eye. We all think that our life is so important, but now you slowly realize the vastness of the universe.

Now it is possible to appreciate every moment in life—every smile and every laugh. Take a moment and picture the gentle breeze on the tree leaves and the subtle movements of nature. Close your eyes and listen to the birds chirping cheerfully as the smell of blossomed flowers is awakening memories of your childhood. Feel the sand and the grass between your fingertips and the rain falling from the sky. Picture yourself gazing deeply into the eyes of a loved one.

We are so small. Time is passing. Our hopes and dreams are put on hold because we are drawn in this drama we call "life." Think of all the ugliness in life and imagine pulling it out. Let it burn on the sun's surface. Set your heart beating to true life. Rise to the consciousness of God. It is in that moment of absolute self-reflection that you can let go of everything you thought you were, becoming everything you truly are. Remember this moment every time someone angers you. Remember this moment every time you are unhappy because you felt cheated.

Put the highest truth in your mind. Don't waste time as your life is precious. Find your inner self and strengthen it. Prepare and build your soul for the journey of leaving this black dot. Now picture yourself holding grains of sand in your palm. Feel their softness and slowly let them slip away. This is just holding you in time. Empty yourself after your self-reflection. Self-realization is the moment you see the truth. How important do you think you are? Over thousands and thousands of years, your life is but a fleeting moment. How will you spend this moment?

Whatever problems you may have, don't let them hold your mind. Everything you thought was important is so small. Let everything you thought you were fade away, and find your inner peace. Experience calmness and clarity from within. Surrender to the depths of meditation. This is the purpose of self-reflection when you have finally let go of everything you thought you were. In your heart you see the truth. There is so much more beyond your existence. You have set yourself free.

All the things you have considered as important are so trivial. They are just here to freeze you in time. Don't let them. Observe the earth pass slowly by the surface of the sun. It is beautiful. Only when you empty yourself can you find the real you and breathe as if it were the first time in your life. Let everything go and in the end you will see love. Only love remains after everything else has faded away. It is that shared consciousness of the universe you have achieved. Breathe deeply, appreciating the moment. Breathe deeply and relax. You are one with the universe.

GUIDED MEDITATION FOR SELF-LOVE

Through this meditation, you will find a way of expressing love towards yourself. This is essential in order to direct love and compassion towards others. Calm down, find your inner peace, boost your self-worth, and care about yourself.

Close your eyes and breathe deeply. You are worthy of love, and you are worthy of loving yourself. Forgive yourself and take care of yourself first so that you can project that to the world around you. Take gentle, relaxed breaths. Inhale through your nose, and let your lungs fill with fresh air. Release slowly and engage in this refreshing cycle of breaths. Sit comfortably and focus on your breathing.

How are you? Are you feeling stressed, anxious or calm? Just allow the thoughts of the past or the worries of the future to melt away. Sit comfortably and be present in the moment. Notice your body as it relaxes. You feel comfortable in the present moment. Feel your eyes relax and unclench your jaw. Relax all those muscles on your face and feel a calming flow of relaxation flowing downwards in your body. Loosen your arms and feel them go limp. Your legs and your entire body feel that gentle, welcoming weight. It's like gravity pulling you down.

Love is such an important expression, but we often neglect to express our love towards ourselves. We must forgive ourselves so that we can be unburdened from the past. Through self-forgiveness, we are able to express love for ourselves and outwards towards others. This will in turn lead to a deeper sense of peace from within. Now, repeat the following mantras. With every mantra you say, you will feel lighter. You will release the tension, and you will allow yourself to float away.

Breathe gently and repeat the following: *"I will allow love for myself. I will accept love from others. I care deeply for others. I will allow forgiveness, and I will forgive myself and others. I am worthy of love, and I am worthy of giving and receiving love."* Now that these mantras are over, continue breathing gently. You are floating away. Feel those muscles of your body from head to toe as they relax even further. Take some deep breaths to release any tension or extra weight that is still within you. As you are exhaling, think of any negative emotion toward yourself and imagine that it is drifting away from you.

Now you are going to repeat these mantras again, believing them to be true beyond any doubt. You will express your feelings, from the bottom of your heart. This love will be unconditional, objective and unlimited. *"I love and accept myself. I am worthy of being loved and I love myself completely. I care about myself and others. I will continue forgiving myself and others in life. I will accept love from others as I deserve to be loved."* Continue breathing deeply, feeling the love in every cell of your body.

Stay in this state of bliss, love, and forgiveness. Feel your heart opening up like a lotus flower, ready to give and receive love. Nurture this flower so that it grows and expands. Feel the love bursting from within you, flowing and spreading to the world. Take deep breaths, relaxing even further. Promise that you will always love and care about yourself. You will be your first priority, no matter what. Only when you have accepted loving yourself can you go ahead with loving others.

If you want, you can repeat the same mantras over and over again until you reach a point where you feel entirely calm, happy, and fulfilled. When you are ready to regain consciousness, count backwards from five. Open your eyes and observe yourself. How are you feeling now? Are you feeling a little bit better than you did before? Repeat this guided meditation every time you are feeling down or questioning yourself. It is a great expression of self-care, allowing you to grow and reach self-awareness.

GUIDED MEDITATION TO FORGIVE YOURSELF

This meditation is suitable for those who have made mistakes in the past and feel tormented by them. It opens the door to self-forgiveness, effectively dealing with negative feelings such as regret and guilt. Some people find it hard to forgive themselves, even for things done a long time ago. However, holding on to guilt helps no one. We must learn to accept and let go.

Pick a time when you are free to relax and meditate, preferably before going to bed. Close your eyes and breathe deeply, inhaling through the nose and exhaling through the mouth. Now imagine the landscape of your dreams. This can be a sandy beach, a green field, a snowy mountain, or a forest. Take a moment and picture its every detail. Now think about yourself. What is it that you want to forgive yourself for? Although it can be painful to bring back this feeling, it is important that you do. This is the only way to toss it away.

Remember that all people make mistakes. If you are suffering from guilt, keep in mind that everyone has experienced the same devastating feelings at least once in their life. Even the finest people have made mistakes because this is only human. Your regrets should not determine your life. Many people have unrealistic expectations of themselves, believing that they should be perfect at all times. However, we are wonderful human beings, and this means that we are bound to make mistakes. These mistakes serve as lessons in life.

You are doing the best you can day by day, and this is something you should congratulate yourself on. There is no point in dwelling on past mistakes. Stressful reactions stem from memories of the past. Take a deep breath and give yourself permission to let go of that memory. Think of the good things that you have done in the past. These definitely outweigh any wrongdoing in your life. Whenever you are feeling down and these negative emotions of regret and guilt creep in, think of something positive you have done in your life.

Spend some time in your dreamy landscape. Listen to the sounds, feel the touch, and experience this beauty. Let the serenity flow into you. Let the absolute tranquility flow into your heart, as this is where your higher self resides. When you are at peace, ask your higher self what you can do to feel better. Ask your higher self to help you. Don't force the answer, as it will come naturally to you. Be mindful and expect the answer. It will show up right away or in the next few days.

Don't beat yourself up for things that happened in the past. Everyone makes mistakes, and it is not in your power to correct them. Nobody has control over the past. What you can do is commit to being better every single day. You can promise the world to work harder and make sure that you do not repeat the same mistakes over and over again. More than that, you can commit towards reaching self-awareness. This will help you see things more clearly.

Remain in your dreamy landscape for as long as you like. Feel your heart filling with love and gratitude for the world. Calm down and forgive yourself. You are a good person, deserving of love and compassion. No one should judge you based on your mistakes. They should concentrate on the amazingly good things that you have done and continue doing. This is how you should think of yourself. Don't feel guilty about something bad that you have done. Focus on the positive things, which are abundant.

When you are ready to come back, start counting backward from five. Take deep breaths and open your eyes. Regain consciousness slowly, without forcing yourself. Feel the benefits of this meditation within your heart and soul. You feel lighter than before, happier, and at peace with any negative feeling you have been suffering from due to mistakes from the past. Continue breathing deeply, slowly, and enjoy the peace around you.

GUIDED MEDITATION FOR SUCCESS

Through this meditation, you will get the opportunity to build the right mindset for success. If you are determined to manifest success, prosperity, and wealth in your life, you need to practice the Law of Attraction.

Begin this guided meditation by sitting comfortably, holding your spine straight, with your palms in your lap facing upwards. Close your eyes and focus awareness on your breathing. Notice how cool and refreshing the air is when you are inhaling through your nose, as well as how warm your breath is as you are exhaling through your mouth. Hold your breath for a few moments as your lungs expand. Exhale with a sigh and feel your body relax. Repeat that for a few more times and then resume normal breathing.

Feel yourself dropping as you become centered and aware of this present moment. You are just now beginning to feel a fire burning within you—a yearning for success. This very fire ignites and excites you. What you are feeling now is an eagerness, or a will to succeed. You are ready to experience success. This fire has prepared you to pursue your deepest desires in life. A tall staircase made of crystal appears before you, leading all the way to the clouds. Imagine yourself taking that very first step, then climbing up the stairs to the destination of your preference.

You begin to feel yourself climbing the stairs effortlessly, with each step feeling easier than the last. As you move upwards, you feel weightless and lift yourself further. As you turn your gaze downwards, you see the world below you. You notice the trees and the mountains, the shores, and the deep blue oceans. Soon, you reach the line of the clouds, and everything around you becomes white. Even though you cannot see the stairs below you, you keep climbing up. You keep rising above the clouds step by step.

Both your heart and soul are filled with determination. Each and every step takes you closer to your dreams, exactly where you belong. Suddenly, you find yourself at the top of the stairs. White light is all around you. This is the time to take a deep breath that fills your lungs with that precious fresh air. Expand your lungs before you exhale gently. You begin to notice that everything around you becomes clearer. The dreams that you had now appear before your eyes and you can touch them. They are your current reality. You are experiencing those dreams. You begin to feel that this is the natural state of things. This is exactly where you are destined to be.

You are experiencing success and a beautiful life that you deserve to be living. Breathe and relax. Remember how effortlessly you have climbed up the stairs since you were meant to be here. Success is not out of reach. In fact, it is the place where you should be living. Start feeling the emotions that derive from this experience. How are you feeling now, having accomplished all your goals and having reached success? Enjoy these feelings so that you can manifest success into your life.

Gradually, your dream reality starts coming down to your physical presence. It seems as though the two realities want to blend in together, allowing you to experience success right now. You are able to allow this dream reality to shower itself into your physical world. It is in your power to live this experience right now. You are in control of your life. Your dream reality is getting lower and lower, almost touching your physical presence. You feel its energy embracing you. Success is your current state, and you feel its benefits overwhelming you. You are successful, accomplished, and content with yourself on all levels.

Continue breathing deeply with your eyes closed for as long as you want this sensation to last. Stay on the top of the world, above the clouds. Enjoy the spectacular view and the amazingly bright light all around you. It is a sight for sore eyes. This is where you are destined to live, feeling exactly the way you do at this very moment. When you are ready, slowly open your eyes and regain consciousness with your surroundings. Take in what you have experienced. Feel these magical, uplifting emotions carrying your inner truth with you wherever you go.

11

THE 30-MINUTE DAILY EMPOWERMENT RITUAL TO SUPERCHARGE SELF-AWARENESS

In the morning, you set the tone for the rest of the day. It is great to be more intentional, since this gives you a clearer perspective and creates a better headspace. By incorporating mindfulness at the start of every day, you will see a great difference in your life. Rather than waking up still feeling lethargic, you will be able to boost your energy levels and actually look forward to your daily challenges.

Through this process, you will become more aware of your surroundings, and you will remain connected to the universe. In this way, you will be mindful of your purpose, and this will help you overcome any natural inclination you may have for procrastination. I know that sometimes all you want to do is crawl back into bed and just stay there. There are times in your life when such a behavioral pattern is perfectly understandable, let alone welcome. However, by indulging in such habits, you prevent yourself from reaching the highest levels of self-growth.

Of course, not all people have the same daily schedule. Some have to wake up really early in the morning and start their day before sunrise. Others tend to wake up later on in the day as they have the luxury to do so. Take a moment and think about your morning habits. Do you use an alarm clock, or do you wake up naturally? Are you relaxed upon waking up, or are you in a hurry? Do you dedicate even a little time for a healthy breakfast or a refreshing shower?

Most people claim that they don't have enough time to dedicate to a morning ritual. So they compromise with a coffee-to-go and leave home in a rush, moments after having gotten out of bed. *"I cannot afford wasting time at breakfast. I've got too much going on in my life right now,"* is an extremely popular justification for their morning chaos. Even if you find that excuse extremely convenient, the truth is that we all have some control over the very beginning of our day. We choose to follow specific habits, either because we don't know how to break them or because we feel they work for us.

If you are determined to change your life, you need to reevaluate your mornings. It would be advisable for you to find the time required to ease yourself into your daily routine. This often means that you have to wake up a little earlier than you used to. I understand that sleep is precious. Nevertheless, you can try going to bed a little earlier too. In this way, you will have the time to rest properly and still awake early the next morning. This is easier said than done, obviously. You can experiment with different sleeping times until you find a pattern that you can follow.

Tidy up the day before, so that you have everything you need without putting much effort. For instance, you are more likely to make breakfast in a clean kitchen. If you wake up and face a pile of dirty dishes, chances are that you will want to avoid washing them in the morning. Instead, you will choose to have a breakfast combo on your way to work. Still, this is counter-productive. Don't get me wrong; I enjoy a cup of coffee and croissants from my favorite place, and I sometimes sit there and work on my laptop. Still, taking the time to prepare your own breakfast is a great way to boost self-awareness and be present in the moment.

You need to organize things in order to adhere to your routine more pleasantly and efficiently. Clean up the kitchen, choose what you are going to wear, and keep everything within reach. If you want, you can also prepare your lunch and have some ingredients for breakfast ready beforehand. This will give you extra motivation to enjoy a hearty, healthy breakfast that nourishes your body and lifts your spirit.

Below I have created a morning ritual, which will help you enhance your self-awareness from the moment you open your eyes. You will establish a deeper connection with the world around you, as well as the decisions you should take within the day. This morning ritual is simple and doable, but you can adjust it to your own personal needs and preferences. Get organized, and let's start your day exactly the way you deserve— as the ideal prelude for wonderful things to happen.

SELF-AWARENESS DAILY RITUAL SECRET FORMULA

First of all, it is important to create a lovely atmosphere at home. This is your shelter, the place you turn to for comfort and security. You need it to be cozy and welcoming, inviting you to relax and let go of any negative emotions. So make sure that you have the perfect space for you to unwind from daily challenges, soothing your body and soul. Some fluffy cushions, cotton sheets, scented candles, and a soft rug will do. Obviously, you are free to decorate your home the way you like. Always pay attention to comfort and aesthetics. However, the most crucial part of creating a welcoming place is cleanliness. Be thorough and meticulous when cleaning. How can you relax in a room that is stuffed with junk, filled with dust and stagnant energy?

Each morning, give yourself some time before checking your phone. I am well aware that your life is busy, and you have so many different tasks to complete. However, take a pause for a few minutes or up to a whole hour after waking up. This is your time. When you check your phone, you will most likely scroll through your emails and get all the notifications you have missed. In turn, you will get stressed and already plan how to respond to these challenges. Furthermore, your phone is associated with mindless activities such as playing games or checking your social media accounts. Don't give in to this temptation, as it is going to distract you.

Another wonderful part of your morning routine should be to let the sunlight in and absorb it for a while. Just open the curtains and let the sun bathe your bedroom. It is amazing how magical this experience can be. Appreciate life and be present in that very moment, allowing yourself to connect with the powerful sun. Open the windows and feel the rejuvenating breeze fondling your cheeks and slightly messing with your hair. I am sure this will make you aware of the moment. This part of your morning is beneficial to your mental and emotional health, not only because of how it makes you feel. It also contributes to balancing your circadian rhythm.

Making your bed is a great way to start your day. Even if you think of this task as trivial, it actually allows you to be mindful of the present moment. It also enables you to complete a task very early in the morning. This adds to your sense of accomplishment. If you are interested in having a productive day ahead, making your bed will set the tone for it. One more reason for making your bed first thing in the morning is that it will prevent you from crawling back in and snoozing. Once you have made your bed, you will instantly feel better. Your personal space will look amazing, neat, and ready to welcome you at nighttime. Have a look around. How does that make you feel when looking at a clean and tidy bedroom?

Take the time to prepare your coffee or tea. Most importantly, take the time to enjoy it. Let the aromas awaken your senses as you are sipping on your liquid bliss. Make some breakfast and eat mindfully. This will help you sustain your body while maintaining that earthy connection. You might notice a difference in the way your breakfast tastes. This is because you are going to appreciate flavors more by drawing your full attention to what you are doing. It is simple yet greatly effective.

Reflect on your goals and intentions for the day early in the morning. You can check your calendar to see what is on your to-do list. Otherwise, you can write down some notes about your plans for the day. This process allows you to be aware of and focused on your goals. Instead of going with the flow and leaving everything to chance, you should try to organize your day properly. In this way, you will prevent getting stressed throughout the day by surprises that might come along or deadlines that you forgot about.

Quite similar to that, you can ask yourself what you want to achieve within your day. This mindfulness meditation only takes a couple of minutes. You can also practice gratitude so that you appreciate your blessings. As a result, you will have a calm, intentional mindset for the rest of the day. It doesn't have to be something too complicated or fancy. Pick what is best for you and get it done. Open your notebook, take a piece of paper, turn on your laptop, or use your phone. Regardless of the method you choose, you should focus on goal-setting and gratitude meditation.

When you are done meditating, you can practice some EFT tapping. This will help you unclog the stagnant energy and clear out the air from any negativity that has been holding you back in life. Tap specific spots on your face and body rhythmically while repeating positive affirmations that enhance your self-worth and set the tone for your day. You need to be confident, so point out how amazing you are and how many great achievements are waiting for you to conquer today. Finally, you can wrap things up with a few minutes of stretching.

In a nutshell, your 30-minute morning ritual should look something like this:

- Get up, let the sunlight in, and make the bed (5 minutes)
- Get a glass of water and prepare breakfast (10 minutes)
- Self-reflect, meditate, and practice gratitude (5 minutes)
- Do EFT tapping to clear limiting beliefs (5 minutes)
- Do stretching (5 minutes)

Once you are done, you will be filled with energy and a positive vibe that is going to last throughout the day. You can work out if you like since it is going to help you get in shape, be present in the moment, and it will elevate your energy. Take a shower if you have sweated it out during your workout, or get dressed and get ready for a fulfilling day ahead. Remember how you are feeling and project that to the world.

Over time, you will notice that your mind has been programmed in a way that allows you to wake up earlier in the morning. This means that you are looking forward to this morning ritual. Even if you feel under the weather, stick to this routine, and you will be rewarded with a more positive look at things in life. Finally, don't forget to smile. Put your widest smile upon your face from the moment you open your eyes because it is, in fact, addictive to smile!

Nighttime Ritual

Your subconscious mind is most impressionable in the evening and particularly the moment right before you fall asleep. All night long, it just soaks up on everything you have programmed it with. Take a moment and think of how you fall asleep. Is it while scrolling on Facebook or Instagram? You need to break this habit as soon as possible. First of all, the light emitted from your phone activates cortisol. This hormone is naturally activated in the morning when you are expected to boost your energy and be productive throughout the day. As a result, you are disrupting your circadian rhythm, and you are having trouble sleeping.

Moreover, the things that you are looking at right before falling asleep influence your subconscious. So if you are scrolling through photos of celebrities and you are comparing yourself to them, this is what your subconscious mind is going to get from you. All night, your subconscious mind will be bombarded with these thoughts of lacking, self-worthlessness, and disappointment.

Instead, what you want to achieve is a positive mentality that will accompany you during your sleep. So it is important that you abstain from such negative stimulants right before going to bed and falling asleep. You can take the time and think about your day. Think of all the wonderful things that you have accomplished. How does that make you feel? Are you proud of yourself? There is nothing noble in being modest. Brag about your achievements and let your subconscious mind know that you are proud of yourself.

When you celebrate yourself and your accomplishments essentially you liberate your body from its deepest suffering. Step into that role and celebrate those things that make you happy every day. Don't shy away from that feeling, as this will determine your subconscious and reprogram your entire existence. If you continue poisoning your mind with negative thoughts and emotions, this is what you are going to project to the world.

Whether you write these thoughts down or you are simply thinking about happy things that have happened throughout the day, you are activating your subconscious mind to seek similarly positive things from now on. You are actually laying the foundation of your future. Think of your subconscious as a goal-setting mechanism, and feed it with whatever you wish to see in your life.

What should your bedtime ritual be like? After having completed your personal hygiene routine, you will be in your comfortable pyjamas, and you will be ready to get under those covers. Make yourself some herbal tea or chamomile, which will allow you to relax and get rid of the tension. Light a scented candle or incense so that your bedroom fills with soothing aromas that will accompany you in your sleep. Take some deep breaths and feel the anxiety leaving your body with each exhale.

Once you feel absolutely relaxed, open your journal. Write down the date and start scribbling without haste. Go through your day and find the things that made you feel proud of yourself. Maybe you were able to deliver an essay in time. Perhaps you helped out as a volunteer on an environmental project. It can be anything, from the way you treated others to milestones in your personal or professional life. Think of all those things and write them down so that you have a visual representation of your day.

Focus on how these things make you feel. Embrace that feeling of happiness, accomplishment, and pride. There is nothing wrong in acknowledging you are awesome. Listen to the encouraging words of others towards you—the praise of your colleagues, the gratitude shown by your parents, or your offspring. Repeat these positive affirmations, directed to you from yourself. *"You are a great leader. You are an inspiration to others. What you did today made me so proud of you. I love you, because you are so compassionate."* These are just a few examples of the amazing affirmations you can use to boost your self-awareness.

By now, you must be feeling great. When you finish writing your list of the things that made you feel good about yourself, count your blessings and express your gratitude. Let your mind drift away in sweet dreams, with that warm sensation of gratitude overwhelming you. If you like, you can have white sounds in the background to help you sleep soundly through the night. As soon as you wake up, open your eyes and observe how you are feeling. I am sure you are already reaping the benefits of a reprogrammed subconscious mind, working towards your self-growth.

AFTERWORD

Now that you have made it to the end of this book, I am so proud of you. You have taken the first step towards reaching your highest purpose in life through a journey of self-discovery and self-actualization. It is amazing that you have the courage and will to try and improve your life because great things are lying ahead for you in life. I am sure that, by now, you have learned how to cope with the challenges of everyday life, overcoming the obstacles that stand in the way and hinder your progress. Hopefully, you will start focusing on yourself and your self-growth, rather than continue to be dragged down by those negative thoughts and insecurities.

Through these chapters, I have referred to several aspects of spiritual awareness and self-improvement. I hope that you have enjoyed reading my book and I hope that it has inspired you to try harder to achieve your goals. Remember that you have the power to change your life, as long as you set your mind to it and stay true to yourself. Don't let any more time pass you by, as this will lead to a prolonged state of idleness. You don't deserve that. Instead, you are entitled to a life of happiness, awareness, growth, prosperity, and spirituality.

It doesn't matter if you have been involved in similar endeavors

AFTERWORD

or not so far in your life. Even without any prior experience, you can do this. You have all the tools you need to discover your true self and find your real purpose. I have broken down the information into chapters, giving you all the resources to further explore your potential. Find the time to care for yourself, and nourish your mind and body. Quiet the distractions, and let go of the toxic people that want to keep you away from your destiny. Your path doesn't involve such distractions.

There will always be excuses justifying a dysfunctional reality. There will always be judgmental people who criticize and bring you down, withholding you from the greatness that you can achieve. Choose what you wish to experience in life. Choose who you want to be and act accordingly. You know how to do that as I have shown you in this book. You know how to attract the things you want and steer clear of the things you don't want to have in your life. According to the Law of Attraction, you can manifest what you want to attract. Take full responsibility for your actions and make them matter.

If you are determined to be a leader, then be one. If your true calling is to teach others, then go ahead and perfect your teaching skills. There are different goals defining your existence, so look really close and find the one that sparks joy within you. No matter what your goal is in life, be persistent and hard-working. Devote your entire existence to this goal until you have mastered everything about it. In this way, you will be able to shine beyond belief and be happy with your life. As a result, others will see you shine and get that powerful inspiration through you to pursue their own dreams and their own fantasies.

Make sure to implement the changes in your lifestyle that are going to shower you with love and appreciation. Instead of sabotaging yourself, you should be reaching for the sky. Every little thing you do in your daily routine should be focused on bringing you closer to your destination. Through the use of guided meditations, EFT tapping sessions, mindfulness, and other techniques, dispose of

AFTERWORD

your baggage and clear out the atmosphere. Make room for the amazing things that are about to unfold before your eyes. Be receiving and grateful for everything that has been brought into your life up to now.

I am sure you are looking forward to this glorious transformation that is about to happen. It is that feeling of intense anticipation that is driving you right now. The excitement you are feeling is a great sign that you are headed in the right direction. You have everything it takes to turn your life around and start living exactly the way you have always dreamed of. Things from now on will be entirely different, and you will be in control of your every day. You have the power to create your own masterpiece. Make it count, make it beautiful, and enjoy living to your fullest potential—you deserve it!

REFERENCES

11417974. (2019, Jan 22). *Mountains Canada Girl* [Photograph]. Pixabay. pixabay.com/photos/mountains-canada-girl-outlook-snow-3959204/.

Akyurt, Engin. (2020, Oct 23). *Woman Model Portrait* [Photograph]. Pixabay. pixabay.com/photos/woman-model-portrait-female-blonde-5674995/.

Bertvthul. (2015, June 22). *The Road Beams Path* [Photograph]. Pixabay. pixabay.com/photos/the-road-beams-path-forest-nature-815297/.

David, Jackson. (2020, Jan 18). *Woman Inspiration Dance* [Photograph]. Pixabay. pixabay.com/photos/woman-inspiration-dance-model-4775733/.

Davis, M. (2019, September 17). *Living the good life*. Big Think. https://bigthink.com/mind-brain/self-actualization-rogers?rebelltitem=4#rebelltitem4

Photos, Free. (2015, Mar 18). *Blonde Girl Backlight* [Photograph]. Pixabay. pixabay.com/photos/blonde-girl-backlight-happy-summer-677779/.

Fotorech. (2017, Aug 21). Sky Freedom Happiness [Photograph].

REFERENCES

Pixabay. pixabay.com/photos/sky-freedom-happiness-relieved-2667455/.

Foundry. (2015, July 30). Woman Meditating Buddhism [Photograph]. Pixabay. pixabay.com/photos/woman-meditating-buddhism-zen-865021/.

Geralt. (2019, Feb 2). *Self Love Heart Diary* [Photograph]. Pixabay. pixabay.com/photos/self-love-heart-diary-hand-keep-3969644/.

Hassan, Mohamed. (2018, Feb 9). *Woman Girl Yoga* [Photograph]. Pixabay. pixabay.com/photos/woman-girl-yoga-relaxation-3141940/.

K, Larisa. (2014, Feb 27). *Tree Flowers Meadow* [Photograph]. Pixabay. pixabay.com/photos/tree-flowers-meadow-tree-trunk-276014/.

Kalyanayahaluwo.(2020, Sept 23). Woman Meditate Healing [Photograph]. Pixabay. pixabay.com/photos/woman-meditate-healing-relax-5596357/.

Kandola, A. (2017, December 20). *Neuro-linguistic programming (NLP): Does it work?* Www.medicalnewstoday.com. https://www.medicalnewstoday.com/articles/320368

Luenen, Michael. (2020, Jan 3). *Freedom Live Love* [Photograph]. Pixabay. pixabay.com/photos/freedom-live-love-nature-cliffs-4737919/.

McLeod, S. (2020, December 29). *Maslow's Hierarchy of Needs*. Simply Psychology; https://www.simplypsychology.org/maslow.html

Mirexa. (2018, Aug 2). *Lavender Nature Flowers* [Photograph]. Pixabay. pixabay.com/photos/lavender-nature-flowers-plants-3576129/.

Moore, C. (2019, April 9). *What Is Mindfulness? Definition + Benefits (Incl. Psychology)*. PositivePsychology.com. https://positivepsychology.com/what-is-mindfulness/

Photos, Free. (2016, July 1). *Happy Woman Smiling* [Photograph]. Pixabay. pixabay.com/photos/happy-woman-smiling-happy-young-1209728/.

Pixel2013. (2017, July 4). Key Heart Feather [Photograph].

REFERENCES

Pixabay. pixabay.com/photos/key-heart-feather-star-pearl-love-2471016/.

Quangpraha. (2017, Dec 17). *The Sea Waterfall Ocean Waves* [Photograph]. Pixabay. pixabay.com/photos/the-sea-the-waterfall-ocean-waves-3018128/.

Saiisha. (2020, March 12). *What Is Your Dharma? Here's How to Find Your True Life Purpose*. YogiApproved™. https://www.yogiapproved.com/life/dharma-find-true-life-purpose/

Skirrow, Gary. (2016, Sept 15). *Yoga Girl Beach* [Photograph]. Pixabay. pixabay.com/photos/yoga-girl-beach-sunset-summer-1665173/.

Sullivan, E. (2019). *Self-actualization*. Encyclopædia Britannica. https://www.britannica.com/science/self-actualization

Tejado, Eva. (2017, Feb 24). *Meditation Numerology Emotional* [Photograph]. Pixabay. pixabay.com/photos/meditation-numerology-2091879/.

Tentis, Dana. (2017, Nov 2). *Beautiful Business Woman* [Photograph]. Pixabay. pixabay.com/photos/beautiful-business-woman-modern-2910260/.

Urban, T. (2013, October 30). *Why Procrastinators Procrastinate — Wait But Why*. Wait but Why. https://waitbutwhy.com/2013/10/why-procrastinators-procrastinate.html

Yogakalyanii. (2018, Sept 2). *Poppies Yoga Field* [Photograph]. Pixabay. pixabay.com/photos/poppies-yoga-field-woman-the-path-3644060/.

YOUR FEEDBACK IS VALUED

From the bottom of my heart, thank you for reading my book. I truly hope that it helps you on your spiritual journey and to live a more empowered and happy life. If it does help you, then I'd like to ask you for a favor. Would you be kind enough to leave an honest review for this book on Amazon? It'd be greatly appreciated and will likely impact the lives of other spiritual seekers across the globe, giving them hope and power. I read **every** review I receive and they help me to become the best writer and spiritual teacher that I can be.

Thank you and good luck!
Angela Grace

Why not join our Facebook community and discuss your spiritual path with like-minded seekers?

We would love to hear from you!

Go here to join the 'Ascending Vibrations' community:
bit.ly/ascendingvibrations

YOUR FREE AUDIOBOOK IS READY

Download the 6+ Hour Audiobook *'Divine Feminine Energy (Manifesting for Women & Feminine Energy Awakening - 2 in 1 Collection)'* Instantly for **FREE!**

If you love listening to audio books on-the-go, I have great news for you. You can download the audio book version of *'Divine Feminine Energy'* for **FREE** just by signing up for a **FREE** 30-day audible trial! See below for more details!

YOUR FREE AUDIOBOOK IS READY

Audible trial benefits

As an audible customer, you'll receive the below benefits with your 30-day free trial:

- Free audible copy of this book
- After the trial, you will get 1 credit each month to use on any audiobook
- Your credits automatically roll over to the next month if you don't use them
- Choose from over 400,000 titles
- Listen anywhere with the audible app across multiple devices
- Make easy, no hassle exchanges of any audiobook you don't love
- Keep your audiobooks forever, even if you cancel your membership
- And much more

Go to the links below to get started:
Go here for AUDIBLE US: bit.ly/divinefeminineenergy
Go here for AUDIBLE UK: bit.ly/divinefeminineenergyuk

www.ingramcontent.com/pod-product-compliance
Lightning Source LLC
Chambersburg PA
CBHW021448070526
44577CB00002B/305